The Book of

BOOKS BY CHARLES HAMILTON

The Book of Autographs
Big Name Hunting: A Beginner's Guide to Autograph Collecting (with Diane Hamilton)
Scribblers and Scoundrels
The Robot That Helped to Make a President
Lincoln in Photographs: An Album of Every Known Pose (with Lloyd Ostendorf)
Collecting Autographs and Manuscripts
Braddock's Defeat
Men of the Underworld: The Professional Criminal's Own Story
Cry of the Thunderbird: The American Indian's Own Story

An Introduction to the Joys and
Techniques of Autograph Collecting
by the World's Foremost Authority

Autographs

by CHARLES HAMILTON

SIMON AND SCHUSTER · NEW YORK

Produced by Lyle Kenyon Engel

Designed by Libra Graphics, Inc.
Manufactured in the United States of America
Printed and bound by The Murray Printing Company
1 2 3 4 5 6 7 8 9 10

Library of Congress Cataloging in Publication Data

Hamilton, Charles, date.
  The book of autographs.

  1. Autographs—Collectors and collecting. I. Title.
Z41.H334   929.8   78-14570

ISBN 0-671-24258-X

Acknowledgments

I am grateful to all the friends who have aided me, and I wish to thank Kenneth W. Rendell of Newton, Massachusetts, and the Stargardt firm of Marburg, Germany, for the use of facsimiles from their handsome catalogues, and Neale Lanigan, Jr., of Fairview Village, Pennsylvania, for his expert assistance in evaluating the autographs of movie stars. I am also indebted to the distinguished author Irving Wallace, to my editor at Simon and Schuster, Peter Schwed, and to Creighton C. Hart of Kansas City, and Doug Beckett and Robert Kuhn of San Francisco, for permission to reproduce autographs from their collections.

Most of all, I wish to thank my wife, Diane, for her tremendous help in reading the manuscript and offering many valuable suggestions.

CHARLES HAMILTON
25 East 77th St.
New York, N.Y. 10021

Contents

By Way of Preface

IN THIS BOOK on the most colorful and exciting of all pursuits, I have set before you the knowledge and experience of more than half a century.

For the first time ever, here is a concise guide to the joys and techniques of autograph collecting, or philography, with hundreds of illustrations and more than five thousand prices. Whatever your interest, you will find it covered in detail.

Celebrities included. In the lists of the famous, I have mixed popular favorites with giants. This explains the presence in the same categories of Edgar A. Guest and Walt Whitman, of Beethoven and Duke Ellington (surely Beethoven would relish the man and his music!), of Rube Goldberg and Michelangelo.

How autographs are evaluated. The values quoted are retail prices, or the amounts you might expect to pay if you purchased from a dealer or at auction. Usually a dealer will offer to buy at about half what he hopes to get, and since he may have to hold a letter or document many years before selling it, this markup is not unreasonable. However, most autographs valued at $20 or less are not of much interest to the average dealer because the high cost of selling makes it hard to realize a profit on inexpensive items.

Abbreviations

First, a definition. The word "autograph" means anything handwritten. It does not necessarily mean *signature.* The following abbreviations are standard among philographers.

Sig.   Signature.

DS   Document signed. A document in the hand of a clerk or typed, but signed by the writer.

LS   Letter signed. A letter in the hand of a clerk or typed, but signed by the writer.

ALS   Autograph letter signed. A letter entirely written and signed by the writer.

AQS   Autograph quotation signed. Usually a verse or statement or a few bars of music written out and signed.

SP   Signed photograph.

A Fresh
Slant on
Handwriting

THE HISTORY OF AUTOGRAPH COLLECTING, OR PHILOGRAPHY

I don't know whether any Roman ever cornered Julius Caesar on the Appian Way, thrust a reed pen into his hand, and demanded his signature on a scrap of papyrus, but I do know that the great Roman orator Cicero prized a handwritten letter of Caesar's in his personal collection. Pliny the Elder eagerly gathered letters and manuscripts of great men, and Suetonius, in his *Lives of the Twelve Caesars*, refers to an archival treasure, "a letter of the Emperor Nero, written in his own hand, now lying before me."

The Romans were philographers rather than autograph seekers. Philography is the science of gathering letters and documents of historic or cultural value, whereas autograph hunting is the hobby of assembling signatures, mere specimens of handwriting and signed photographs of celebrities. Many collectors enjoy both pursuits at the same time. There are about 15,000 philographers in America and around three million autograph seekers.

The hobby of signature collecting began in the sixteenth century, in Germany, where students at the universities made a practice of carrying albums in which their friends wrote out and signed classical quotations or made little sketches. Then, in the early eighteenth century, there was a revival of the ancient science of philography, and a few scholars began to gather historical and literary letters and manuscripts.

By the mid-nineteenth century the two pursuits flourished concurrently, even as they do today.

THE IMPORTANCE OF PHILOGRAPHY

You may, if you wish, look upon autograph letters and documents as mere sentimental relics of great men and women, but I prefer to regard them as the whole basis of our history and culture. Without old letters and manuscripts there could be no recorded history. Who could understand a great battle without reading the letters and diaries of the men who fought in it? Who could publish an accurate text of Wagner without studying his original manuscripts, or the poems of Keats without reviewing every line just as it came from his quill?

It is fascinating to reflect that John Heming and Henry Condell, Shakespeare's friends, may have used the original prompt books and very likely the original manuscripts of the great dramatist when they compiled the first folio of his plays and poems. If these manuscript sources ever turn up, it will be the greatest philographic discovery of all time.

1. *William Shakespeare*

Autograph letters and documents are the most intimate and self-proving of all relics. They were not only touched by the great, but they represent the very thoughts, even the very words, of the illustrious men and women of the past.

How dull of heart and empty of soul must be the man or woman who could hold an original letter of Lincoln and not feel a quickening of the pulse, a sudden kinship with the writer.

Philography is a pursuit for all who love romance and excitement.

WHAT MAKES AN AUTOGRAPH VALUABLE

Nearly every day some visitor bursts into my gallery with the news: "I've just discovered in my attic an ancient parchment document nearly three hundred years old!"

And I explain, as tactfully as I can: "It's not the age of a letter or document that makes it valuable. Only documents dated before the year 1400 are valued solely for their age. Two- or three-hundred-year-old property deeds or legal contracts on parchment are so abundant and inexpensive that the most one can say for them is that they make excellent lampshades. Value is based upon demand, and there is almost no demand for old deeds."

But just yesterday a young man was chatting with me. "I know where there's a little handwritten letter of President Kennedy on White House stationery," he said casually. "Does it have any value?"

"About three thousand dollars," I said. "Kennedy's handwritten presidential letters are extremely rare."

"My gosh!" he exclaimed. "Why, it's just sitting in a file like any worthless old piece of paper. I had no idea it had any value."

The demand for handwritten—not typed—letters of recent presidents, especially letters written during the presidency, is new in the history of philography. Hand-penned letters *as president* of Franklin D. Roosevelt,

Eisenhower, Johnson or Nixon are worth more than comparable letters of Washington or Lincoln.

Letters with important or interesting contents are especially sought. You can buy a parchment military commission signed by Lincoln for about $850, but an eyewitness account of Lincoln's assassination by someone unknown to fame might be worth two or three times that sum.

Letters and documents are worth much more than mere signatures, and the *rarity* of an autograph, strangely enough, is often not an important factor in its value. Letters signed by Napoleon are extremely abundant—he signed countless thousands of them—yet the demand is always present, and such letters fetch from $250 to $2500, depending upon their historical significance. Letters of Freud and Einstein are common, but the

demand is so keen that their value is considerable. Handwritten letters of Faulkner and Hemingway, dead less than a generation, are worth much more than comparable letters of Dickens and Thackeray. But demand is based upon fashion and fashion is fickle. Fifty years ago letters of Lloyd George were eagerly sought. Today the vogue is for Sir Winston Churchill. Forty years ago literary collectors were wild for Arnold Bennett and James Branch Cabell. Now they are wild for James Joyce and F. Scott Fitzgerald.

THE SOURCES OF AUTOGRAPHS

Sources for dealers. Autographs come to dealers and auctioneers from private estates and from collectors. Almost every day I buy several private collections and get additional collections consigned for auction. Often letters which I sold many years ago return to me after passing through many hands, and I recognize them as old friends. Faces and names of collectors and vendors slip instantly out of my mind, but once I have set eyes upon a document I rarely, if ever, forget it.

Ten years ago a woman handed me a letter of F. Scott Fitzgerald and asked, "What will you give me for this?" I glanced at the letter, a rather unimportant one but in fine condition.

"One hundred dollars," I said.

The woman replied with the stock answer of comparison shoppers. "I'll have to ask my husband and see what he thinks."

About five years later she was back and produced a worn envelope from her purse. I did not recognize the woman but I recognized the letter, or rather, what was left of it. The owner had opened and folded it so often in her quest for the highest price that it was now in three pieces. "What will you give me for this?" she asked.

"Fifty dollars," I said.

"Why," she protested, "last time you offered one hundred dollars and now it's five years older and worth more."

I have little patience with people who wittingly damage historical documents. "Madam," I observed, "you have peddled this letter from here to Canarsie and you have worn it out. If you continue for another five years, my offer will be ten dollars."

The woman elevated her nose and put the envelope back in her purse. I've often wondered what she finally did with this holographic jigsaw puzzle.

Sources for collectors. The most obvious and simple source for a beginner is the celebrity himself, who may be approached either in person or by mail. Many noted people are, for excellent reasons, hostile to signature hunters. Paul Newman and Neil Armstrong, for example, look with a steely-eyed scowl upon sidewalk predators. However, if Armstrong is solicited by mail, he may respond with a signed photograph. But be sure to enclosed a stamped, self-addressed envelope when you write to him or any other celebrity.

Collecting signatures in an album or on index cards or magazine covers is the most rudimentary and least interesting form of autograph seeking. It is advisable, when writing to noted persons, to ask them a question, such as "What was your favorite subject in high school?" or "Who in your opinion is the greatest man who ever lived?" or some similar provocative inquiry. The replies you receive will be fascinating to read and possibly valuable. When you begin a collection like this you will be taking your first step from autograph seeking toward philography.

HOW TO COLLECT FOR INVESTMENT OR PROFIT

"How can I be sure my collection will increase in value?" is the question most often put to me by collectors, and it is the hardest to answer. Short of being psychic, there's no way to guarantee financial success in either philography or signature hunting. Nevertheless, there are some important steps you can take:

1. Buy from as many sources as possible until you find the source (dealer or auction) that suits you best.

2. Always buy the finest material you can afford. Rather than assembling a hodge-podge of inexpensive notes and signatures, get fine and interesting letters.

3. Buy your autographs from reliable sources and avoid private sellers, small auction houses and flea markets. Otherwise you may find yourself with a worthless collection of facsimiles and forgeries.

4. If you write to celebrities, try to get interesting replies, not mere signatures on index cards or *Time* covers.

10

Der Oberste Befehlshaber
der Wehrmacht

Hauptquartier, den 7.5.45.

/Bitte in der Antwort vorstehendes
Geschäftszeichen, das Datum und
kurzen Inhalt anzugeben./

ICH BEVOLLMÄCHTIGE

GENERALFELDMARSCHALL   K E I T E L

ALS CHEF DES OBERKOMMANDOS DER

WEHRMACHT UND ZUGLEICH ALS OBER-

BEFEHLSHABER DES HEERES,

GENERALADMIRAL VON FRIEDEBURG

ALS OBERBEFEHLSHABER DER KRIEGSMARINE,

GENERALOBERST   S T U M P F

ALS VERTRETER DES OBERBEFEHLSHABERS

DER LUFTWAFFE

ZUR RATIFIZIERUNG DER BEDINGUNGSLKSEN KAPITULATION

DER DEUTSCHEN STREITKRAFTE GEGENUBER DEM OBERBEFEHLSHABER

DER ALLIIERTEN EXPEDITIONSSTREITKRAFTE UND DEM SOWJET-OBER-

KOMMANDO.

DÖNITZ
GROSSADMIRAL

10. *Doenitz's orders to surrender the German armed forces, May 7, 1945. A souvenir copy, signed by Doenitz and Eisenhower. Eisenhower usually refused to put his signature on the same page with a Nazi but was persuaded to sign this transcript by the noted philographer, Congressman Seymour Halpern.*

5. Should you care to speculate, you might gamble on who will be the next President or try to pick the authors who will be considered the great writers a decade from now. I once invested heavily in Thomas E. Dewey "futures" when he was certain, I thought, to be elected President. Truman pulled an upset, and I sold my collection of Dewey letters for a fraction of what I had paid. This experience made me wary, and some years later I passed up several chances to buy at low prices a handful of outstanding John F. Kennedy letters during his campaign debates with Nixon.

There is certainly money, and lots of it, to be made in autograph speculation, and I know many who have done it. But, as you can see, I am not the one from whom you should seek advice.

SERENDIPITY, THE SURPRISE INGREDIENT IN COLLECTING

Sooner or later most collectors have a delightful encounter with serendipity, the art of discovering great things in unexpected places. Many small dealers, known in the trade as "knockers" or "scouts," are blessed by the stars of Serendip and seem constantly to turn up rarities. I know a man who bought a cardboard carton at auction for a few dollars and then discovered it contained 140 letters of Mark Twain. He sold the collection for $20,000. In the last century, an Englishman seeking birds' eggs climbed a tree and discovered a rare document of Richard III in a magpie's nest. The bird, it turned out, had found the old paper in the open-windowed attic of a nearby mansion and carried it off.

I was once journeying to Boston with my wife, Diane, and while in the club car of the train I mentioned to a stranger that I was an autograph expert. A porter overheard me and took from his pocket a ragged album.

11

11. *Richard III (Ricardus Rex)*

12. *Quatrain written out and signed by Robert Frost*

12

He allowed me a quick peek at *one word only* from something penned in the album. "Let's see if you really are an expert," he grinned. "Who wrote that word?"

"Robert Frost," I said.

The porter gasped with amazement. Then he showed me a whole quatrain written and signed by the celebrated poet, explaining that Frost had written out the poem years before while traveling on the train.

The porter sold the page to me for my offer of $100 in cash and, upon alighting from the train at Boston, I turned it over to a collector who met me at the station for $150, slightly less than its retail value.

In June, 1977, I was visiting Westhampton Beach with my wife, looking for a suitable house to buy or rent for the summer. We found an old home, built in 1926, which was interesting enough to merit a closer examination. As Diane and I strolled through its library with the real estate agent, I cast my eyes around quickly at the two or three thousand leather-bound volumes, similar to those which comprise any gentleman's library. My gaze suddenly fell upon a battered volume in a dark corner. I crossed the room and pulled it from the bottom shelf, at the same time blowing a cloud of dust from it. In faded letters it bore on the spine the words "Revolutionary Autographs. Vol. II." I must confess that my hands trembled slightly with excitement as I opened the worn old volume, probably for the first time in half a century. Inside, it glowed with the glories of American history. Here were hundreds of letters, many of them addressed to John Jay, of Franklin, John Adams, Paul Revere, John Hancock, Jefferson, Benedict Arnold, George Washington, Nathanael Greene—all of them dated during the Revolution. I was thrilled and elated, and within two weeks, after a brief and pleasant negotiation with the owner, the precious volume was mine.

13. *Paul Revere*

13

Later I learned that it was a stray volume from a three-volume set compiled in 1884. Volume I had been presented to an historical society many years earlier, Volume III had vanished, and serendipity had led me to the chance discovery of Volume II, one of the greatest finds of my career.

VALUE OF CONTEMPORARY AUTOGRAPHS

Generally, the signatures and letters of living persons are not especially valuable, but there are many exceptions. Those of presidents and other outstanding political leaders, noted authors and legendary movie stars are much sought. And these autographs are the ones which are usually hardest to get.

Occasionally celebrities have the hardihood to ask me the value of their signatures. Not long ago I ran into Joey Adams in a restaurant, surrounded by a group of friends, and he said, "How is my autograph doing these days, Charles?"

"Good news, Joey," I replied. "It's gone up to thirty-five cents."

Joey mustered a laugh, and I added, "But that's only if it's written in green ink."

The late Joe Pyne, noted for his vitriolic interviews, had been castigating me on his television show for about ten minutes. Then he paused and boldly inquired about the value of his signature. I revenged myself by saying, "Speak to me privately about it after we get off the air."

Pyne took my jest good-naturedly. "As bad as that, eh?"

HOW TO PRESERVE YOUR COLLECTION

The best way to preserve a signature or letter or document is to leave it alone. If you wish, put it in a manila folder or between sheets of transparent acetate, available at any stationery store. Here are some very important *don'ts*:

1. Don't paste or glue any autograph down, and don't repair it with Scotch tape.
2. Don't hang it near a bright light or in the sun if you frame it.
3. Don't trim it or cut it.
4. Don't keep it in a very damp or very hot place.

If you follow these simple rules, your collection will remain in excellent condition for the next thousand years.

TRAPS FOR THE UNWARY

Without the forgeries, facsimiles, proxy and autopen signatures, gathering a collection would lose much of its piquancy. These pitfalls add zest and excitement to the chase.

Forgeries. Almost every signature worth collecting has been forged.

14   15

16 (signature of Washington)

17 (signature of Washington)

SOME CELEBRATED FORGERIES

14. *Signature of William Shakespeare*

15. *Forgery of Shakespeare by Ireland*

16. *Signature of Washington*

17. *Forgery of Washington by Spring*

18. *Signature of Lincoln*

19. *Forgery of Lincoln by Cosey*

20. *Signature of Adolf Hitler*

21. *Forgery of Hitler by Sutton*

18 (signature of Lincoln) 19 (signature of Lincoln)

20  21

There was a forger in the 1790s—William Henry Ireland—who turned out Shakespeares that fooled even the British Museum. Another forger in the 1860s—Robert Spring—specialized in George Washington. In the 1930s, Joseph Cosey, a forger, manufactured scores of Lincolns that are still on the market. And just last year I exposed the activities of Arthur Sutton, whose many forgeries of movie stars, Adolf Hitler and John F. Kennedy had glutted private collections.

How can you identify a forgery? Usually, somewhere in the equation, the forger trips up and gets a fact wrong or uses the wrong paper or the wrong ink or makes an incorrect flourish or two in the signature. But the best way to avoid forgeries is to buy from an expert.

Proxy signatures. At some time or another, nearly every busy man allows a secretary to sign his mail for him. I once had at the same time three secretaries who imitated my signature on letters.

The first to use proxy signatures extensively were the kings of France, especially Louis XIV to Louis XVI. When Napoleon was first consul, his aide, Maret, signed routine documents for him. The presidents from Andrew Jackson to Theodore Roosevelt employed secretaries to counterfeit their signatures on land grants. After 1834 no president personally signed such documents. Today the president puts his name on virtually no letters and very few official papers.

22. *Napoleon (as Bonaparte) and his proxy signer. The signature of Bonaparte can be identified by the flourish which Napoleon put under all his signatures.*

In the film studios from 1920 to 1960 there were regular factories of skilled penmen who forged the signatures of movie stars on photographs, many with personal inscriptions. Sometimes thousands of photos "signed" by a single star would be mailed out in the course of a week. Jean Harlow's mother signed photos and even wrote entire letters for her famous daughter.

23. *Signature of Jean Harlow written by her mother*

24. *Authentic signature of Jean Harlow*

Facsimiles. When King George V of England wrote a letter welcoming the American soldiers landing in France during World War I, had it printed in facsimile on his engraved stationery, and distributed it to our entire army, he launched a thousand hopefuls who have journeyed to my gallery in the belief that they own the original in the king's hand. They are crushed when I tell them it is worth only about a dollar.

Other omnipresent facsimiles are Lincoln's letter to Mrs. Bixby, Churchill's or Charles de Gaulle's thanks for congratulations or good wishes, acknowledgments by Hoover or Truman of birthday greetings, and typed letters soliciting funds signed by Einstein or Helen Keller.

"Wrong" men. There were dozens of John Adamses living in Massachusetts at the same time as the President, and occasionally these carpenters and farmers and joiners are confused with him. Most such "wrong" men and women are easily identified by their handwriting or the contents of their letters.

Autopen signatures. The most difficult of all signature traps to spot is the autopen signature, since it is written with pen and ink and exactly

25   Sincerely,

25. *Machine (or robot) signatures of John F. Kennedy, Richard Nixon and Gerald R. Ford*

duplicates the original signature of the writer. To identify an autopen signature you must be familiar with the pattern. Except for slight variations, every signature from a given pattern is identical, and each can be superimposed over every other one. Unfortunately for collectors, it is easy to create new patterns. Nixon used several dozen patterns during his career, fourteen of them while he was President. Kennedy used only seven, but Jimmy Carter will undoubtedly break all records, for I have already seen many different patterns on his letters from the White House.

The autopen is widely used by politicians and world leaders and by astronauts and cosmonauts.

An even greater problem is posed by the Signa-Signer, a recent invention which can write a complete short letter. The person using the machine merely pens a brief letter, signs it, and the Signa-Signer is ready instantly to reproduce it in large quantities. If the president wishes to invite 100 senators to a ball, he merely scribbles a note to "Dear Senator," and 100 informal letters, all handwritten, will be turned out and mailed to senators, each of whom is flattered that a man as busy as the President took time to write him a personal note.

HOW TO SELL YOUR AUTOGRAPHS

There is an eager market for interesting letters and documents, manuscripts, diaries and journals, and even mere signatures of famous men and women. Letters of Civil War soldiers, slave deeds, whaling logs, unusual or significant letters of any kind are much desired. They can be sold two ways.

At auction. Selling at auction is always a gamble, but one which may pay off handsomely. Last year a woman brought me an old journal written by a member of Commodore Perry's expedition to Japan. She had found it in an attic. As I had never handled anything quite like it before, I hesitated to make a cash offer. I advised the owner to let me sell it on her behalf at my next auction at the Waldorf-Astoria. I estimated its value at $750, but I felt that it might bring as much as $1000. After an exciting session of spirited bidding, the manuscript was knocked down for a resounding $4500.

When a sale is made at auction, the Hamilton Galleries charges a set commission, for which it handles all details, such as cataloguing, illustrating (if desirable) and insurance, as well as the collection of payment from the auction buyer.

Outright sale. If you elect to dispose of your autographs by outright sale, you will be paid immediately in cash and you will know exactly what sum you will get. There are many dealers who buy autographs, and all reliable dealers will make offers, provided you are willing to accept or reject the offer. It is considered improper to conduct "private auctions," traveling from one dealer to another in an effort to jack up the offer, but it is perfectly proper to say no to any offer you find unsatisfactory. Reputable dealers make honest and fair offers and withdraw any offer which is not promptly accepted.

Charles Hamilton Galleries, Inc., not only sells autographs at auction but also spends tens of thousands of dollars in cash every year for autographs. If you would like a free brochure entitled *How to Sell Your Autographs*, just write to me.

Charles Hamilton

CHARLES HAMILTON
25 East 77th St.
New York, N.Y. 10021

The "Most" in Famous Signatures

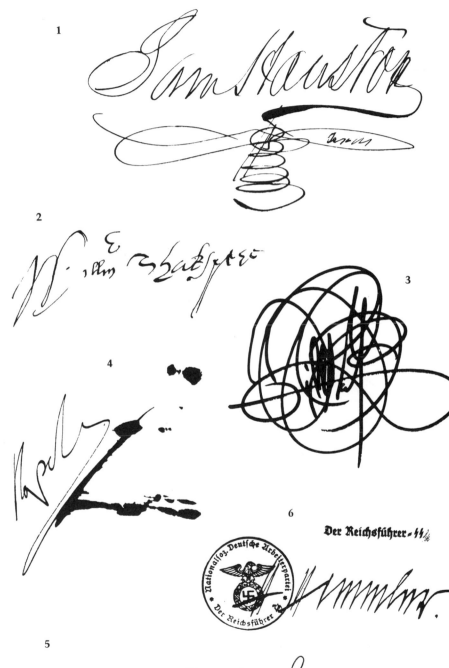

1. *Most egotistical signature: Sam Houston, Texan patriot. Because of the flamboyant way he wrote* **Sam**, *his enemies called him "the great 'I am' Houston."*

2. *Most valuable signature: William Shakespeare, English dramatist. I'll pay $1 million for one.*

3. *Most illegible signature: (William B. Camp, Comptroller of the Currency. It looks like a fishing line after a bad cast.*

4. *Most blotted signature: Napoleon I, Emperor of France. And afterward, he wiped his quill on his white doeskin pants.*

5. *Most disputed signature: Howard Hughes, American billionaire. But this example is not disputed!*

6. *Most feared signature: Heinrich Himmler, Gestapo chief. It resembles a row of fixed bayonets.*

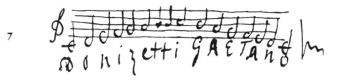

7

7. *Most bizarre signature: Gaetano Donizetti, Italian composer. You can play it on your piano—or sing it.*

8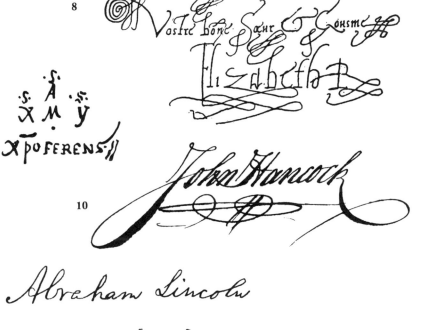

8. *Most regal signature: Elizabeth I, Queen of England. It's a study in courtly elegance and suggests her famed "Queen Elizabeth" ruff.*

9

9. *Most cryptic signature: Christopher Columbus, Italian explorer. Because the signature forms a Jewish triangle and incorporates several Hebrew letters, many experts say it proves that Columbus was a Jew.*

10

10. *Most famous signature: John Hancock, American patriot. Signed large on the Declaration of Independence so that "King George won't have to put on his spectacles to read it," the name is now a synonym for the word "signature."*

11

11. *Most sought-after signature: Abraham Lincoln, American president. It's as plain and homespun as the man himself.*

12

12. *Most fanciful signature: George Cruikshank, English artist, illustrator of Dickens. It's a miniature fairyland peopled by musical elves.*

13

13. *Most graphic occupational signature: Richard Petty, champion auto racer. It incorporates no less than eleven racetracks.*

Entertainment Personalities of the Past

JOHN BARRYMORE ENJOYED DRINKING and was not particular about where he drank. One afternoon as he stood, glass in hand, at a seedy waterfront bar he noticed a burly, evil-looking stranger staring at him. The man was unkempt and unshaven, and his fierce look alarmed Barrymore. Finally the man swaggered over to the actor, reached suddenly into his pocket, whipped out a pen and asked meekly, "May I have your autograph, Mr. Barrymore?" The greatly relieved actor complied.

W. C. Fields often hurled imprecations at autograph hounds but his oaths were always amusingly erudite. Errol Flynn went further. When a traffic cop pursued him and ordered him to pull over to the curb just to get his signature, the actor exploded. The cop was so incensed that he threw Flynn in the local slammer to cool off.

1. *John Barrymore*

2. *Errol Flynn*

3. *W. C. Fields*

4. *Lola Montez*

It is the actors and actresses and entertainers who have led scandalous or romantic lives who especially appeal to autograph collectors. You will find a bust of Charlotte Cushman in the Hall of Fame at Columbia, but I have not even listed that virtuous actress here, although her letters do sell for a few dollars. But you will find in my list that beautiful, immodest, outrageous upsetter of kingdoms and instigator of duels, Lola Montez. Her life reads like fiction and her letters are often exciting. I once had a letter of Lola in which she threatened to horsewhip a critic.

Among movie stars, the colorful Rudolph Valentino is especially sought. His letters and signed photos are very rare. I recall a series of letters, penned in Italian to a boyhood friend when Valentino was only fifteen, in which the future actor admitted he had acquired a social disease from a chorus girl, adding, "From now on, I go out only with nice girls."

5

Cordially yours,

Rudolph Valentino

5. *Rudolph Valentino*

Interest in movie stars has enormously increased during the past three or four years, and they now vie with the Presidents in popularity among collectors. There is no doubt that letters and signed photos of the legendary personalities will continue to grow in value.

* See key to abbreviations, p. 11.

	SIG.	DS/LS	ALS	AQS	SP *
Fred Allen	$10	$20	$35	$25	$25
Phineas T. Barnum	15	40	60	50	100
Ethel Barrymore	15	25	35	20	40
John Barrymore	35	50	90	75	85
Lionel Barrymore	15	25	35	20	40
Wallace Beery	10	25	45	25	50
Sarah Bernhardt	15	35	50	35	100
Jussi Bjoerling	8	20	30	15	30
Humphrey Bogart	35	60	100	75	100
Edwin Booth	20	50	75	50	100
Junius Brutus Booth	25	75	100	75	200
Fanny Brice	10	20	30	20	40
Billie Burke	10	20	35	25	30
Eddie Cantor	8	15	35	20	30
Enrico Caruso	45	85	100	75	125
Feodor Chaliapin	35	65	85	75	100
Lon Chaney	75	150	200	100	300
Lon Chaney, Jr.	20	40	75	50	100
Charles Chaplin	25	50	75	50	75
Gary Cooper	20	25	65	45	60
Katharine Cornell	8	15	35	20	20

	SIG.	DS/LS	ALS	AQS	SP *
Noel Coward	$ 12	$ 35	$ 50	$ 35	$ 50
Joan Crawford	10	15	40	20	25
Bing Crosby	10	15	25	20	20
Cecil B. DeMille	8	15	50	25	35
Marie Dressler	15	35	50	35	75
Isadora Duncan	35	65	125	100	200
Eleanora Duse	50	100	200	150	200
Douglas Fairbanks, Sr.	12	25	45	35	75
W. C. Fields	35	65	100	100	150
Errol Flynn	20	50	75	50	75
Edwin Forrest	15	25	65	50	75
Clark Gable	40	75	125	100	150
Amelita Galli-Curci	15	35	50	35	50
Judy Garland	45	75	100	75	125
William Gillette	10	20	40	30	40
Samuel Goldwyn	8	15	35	25	30
D. W. Griffith	35	75	120	75	100
Yvette Guilbert	15	35	50	35	70
Oliver Hardy	15	30	65	30	75
William S. Hart	12	30	50	35	75
Anna Held	20	35	50	35	75
Harry Houdini	30	75	150	100	125
Leslie Howard	15	30	50	30	50
Henry Irving	6	10	20	15	50
Al Jolson	30	65	100	75	100
Boris Karloff	20	50	85	50	100
Buster Keaton	10	25	50	35	85
Lily Langtry	15	45	75	50	75
Harry Lauder	8	15	25	20	25
Charles Laughton	10	25	45	25	50
Stan Laurel	15	30	65	30	75
Jenny Lind	15	40	65	50	200
Harold Lloyd	10	25	45	25	45
Carole Lombard	35	50	75	50	100
Bela Lugosi	20	45	75	50	100
Jeanette MacDonald	10	25	50	25	50
Fredric March	8	15	25	15	20
Chico Marx	15	35	75	50	75
Groucho Marx	20	40	90	75	75
Harpo Marx	15	35	75	50	75
Nellie Melba	12	30	50	30	75
Glenn Miller	25	50	75	50	75
Tom Mix	12	25	50	25	65
Marilyn Monroe	50	100	200	100	250

	SIG.	DS/LS	ALS	AQS	SP *
Lola Montez	$60	$150	$300	$175	$350
Vaslav Nijinsky	50	150	300	150	750
Anna Pavlova	25	75	150	75	100
Tyrone E. Power	12	25	50	25	50
Elvis Presley	60	100	260	120	200
Basil Rathbone	15	30	50	30	75
Paul Robeson	15	30	50	30	75
Will Rogers	25	50	85	50	85
Lillian Russell	15	30	75	50	100
E. Schumann-Heink	15	30	50	35	70
Robert Taylor	10	25	50	25	50
Ellen Terry	8	15	35	15	50
Arturo Toscanini	25	50	100	75	100
Spencer Tracy	10	30	50	30	50
Rudolph Valentino	75	120	275	120	300
Paul Whiteman	10	30	50	30	65

6. *Fred Allen*

7. *Edwin Booth*

8. *Wallace Beery*

9. *Gary Cooper*

10. *Feodor Chaliapin*

11. *Charlie Chaplin (original sketch)*

6

8

7

9

11

10

12

13

14

15

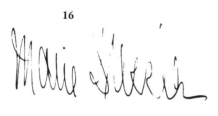

16

17

19

18

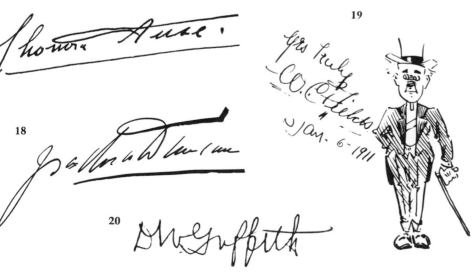

20

12. *Cecil B. DeMille*

13. *Humphrey Bogart*

14. *Joan Crawford*

15. *Enrico Caruso (self-portrait)*

16. *Marie Dressler*

17. *Eleanora Duse*

18. *Isadora Duncan*

19. *W. C. Fields (self-portrait)*

20. *D. W. Griffith*

21

22

23

24

25

26

27

28

Samuel Goldwyn

29

30

31

32

33. Carole Lombard (Gable)

31. William Gillette

32. Yvette Guilbert

33. Carole Lombard (Gable)

34. Boris Karloff

35. Harold Lloyd

36. Groucho Marx

37. Spencer Tracy

38. Tyrone Power

39. Robert Taylor

33

34

35

I'm an American ham, who loves Canadian bacon

Cordially

Groucho Marx

36

37

38

39

40. *Basil Rathbone*

41. *Harry Lauder (self-portrait)*

42. *Jenny Lind*

43. *Jeanette MacDonald*

44. *Marilyn Monroe*

45. *Will Rogers*

46. *Bela Lugosi*

47. *Vaslav Nijinsky*

48. *Lon Chaney, Sr. (original pencil sketch by Margery Browne, signed by Chaney)*

Frontiersmen
and Indians

MOST OF THEM made their reputations with guns and knives. Many of them died violently. They wrote few letters and some, like Jim Bridger, Calamity Jane and Red Jacket, could sign only with an X. Such Xs come high on the autograph market, however, for the lore of the Old West has an immense appeal to philographers.

Calamity her *Jane*
1. mark

2. *Sitting Bull*

3. *Very Respectfully*
P. F. Garrett

4. *Chief Joseph, ✝ His mark*
Washington DC.
Feb. 1903
Andrew Whitman,
Interpreter

1. *Calamity Jane*

2. *Sitting Bull*

3. *Pat Garrett*

4. *Chief Joseph*

The most colorful signatures are those of the Indians. Geronimo printed his signature sideways from the top down and it looked like a totem. Sitting Bull learned to write his name the white man's way so he could sign autographs for a dollar at Buffalo Bill's Wild West Show. Chief Joseph never learned to write at all, and the only signatures other than Xs which survive are crude copies of his name, with many letters incorrectly formed, based on signatures provided as models by white men.

The sheriffs of the frontier are an intriguing group. Rarest is Wild Bill Hickok, and most abundant—though far from common—is Pat Garrett, slayer of Billy the Kid.

* See key to abbreviations, p. 11.

	SIG.	DS/LS	ALS *
Judge Roy Bean	$150	$450	$750
Daniel Boone	500	2000	6500
James Bowie	300	800	2500
Joseph Brant	200	450	1200
James Bridger	—	2500	—
Calamity Jane (Martha Jane Burke)	—	2500	—
Kit Carson	275	650	—
William Clark	150	300	525
William Frederick "Buffalo Bill" Cody	65	100	225
David Crockett	300	625	1500
George A. Custer	300	650	1200
Wyatt Earp	150	400	1000
William G. Fargo	60	75	275
Pat Garrett	100	150	475
Geronimo	800	—	—
Wild Bill (J. B.) Hickok	450	2500	5000
Ben Holladay	50	150	250
Sam Houston	150	325	450
Chief Joseph	800	—	—
Meriwether Lewis	350	625	850
Manuel Lisa	75	325	600
James W. Marshall	350	—	—
Bat Masterson	150	350	800
Frank North	50	150	250
Annie Oakley	85	175	425
King Philip	—	3500	—
Zebulon Pike	50	165	300
Allan Pinkerton	60	100	225
Pontiac	—	4500	—
Red Jacket	—	500	—
John Ross	100	160	300
Sequoya (George Guess)	—	1500	3500
Junípero Serra	300	1000	4500
John Sevier	50	175	575
Sitting Bull	850	—	—
John A. Sutter	150	350	550
William Barret Travis	—	350	2500
Conrad Weiser	50	150	250
Henry Wells	60	75	275
Eleazer Williams	50	120	250

5 *Sir the 2000 acres of Land you are to make me a titel to out of your 5000 acres I have Sold to Mr James Parbery and Desire you Would Make him a Deed to the Same on aplecation your Complyence Will Much oblyge your omble Servent*

To Mr gadis Winston

Test
John Fowler
Elias Bastin
Hiram Harrison

Daniel Boone

May the 9th 1786

5. *Daniel Boone (autograph letter signed)*

6. *Buffalo Bill (autograph quotation signed)*

7. *George A. Custer*

8. *James Bowie*

9. *Joseph Brant*

10. *Kit Carson*

11. *William Clark*

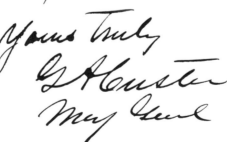

James Bowie

8

True to friend & foe
W F Cody
6 *Buffalo Bill*
1887

7 *Yours Truly*
G A Custer
Maj Genl

9 *Jos. Brant*

10 *Kit Carson*

11 *Wm Clark*

12. *David Crockett*

13. *Wyatt Earp*

14. *William G. Fargo*

15. *J. B. "Wild Bill" Hickok*
(autograph note signed)

16. *W. B. "Bat" Masterson*

17. *Annie Oakley*

18. *Allan Pinkerton*

19. *King Philip*

20. *Geronimo*

21. *Red Jacket*

22. *Chief Joseph*

23. *Meriwether Lewis*

24. *Manuel Lisa*

25. *James W. Marshall (special card signed)*

26. *Zebulon Pike*

27. *John Ross*

28. *Junípero Serra*

29. *John Sevier*

30. *John A. Sutter*

31. *Henry Wells*

32. *Sitting Bull (pictographic signature)*

33. *Eleazer Williams*

World Statesmen and Political Leaders

IT IS A CURIOUS fact that the autograph letters and documents of violent leaders are most always rarer and more desirable than those of statesmen who lead placid lives. Idi Amin's letters are much rarer and far more valuable than those of Anthony Eden. The collector will have no trouble finding an autograph of the Dalai Lama or Thomas E. Dewey, but Stalin and Trotsky, those men of dark mystery and intrigue, may long elude his portfolio.

1. *Jean Paul Marat*

2. *Maximilien Robespierre*

3. *Dalai Lama*

4. *Leon Trotsky*

5. *Fidel Castro*

Collectors delight in gory relics. A bloodstain on a document can add hundreds, even thousands, of dollars to its value. Still in existence are the blood-soaked document that Marat was perusing in his bathtub when Charlotte Corday plunged a dagger into his bosom, and the death warrant to which Robespierre had affixed only the first two letters of his signature when the bullet of an insurgent struck his chest and splattered the paper with his blood. These gruesome souvenirs are among the great national treasures of France.

Fidel Castro may not qualify as a philographer but he is keenly interested in the monetary value of autographs, and one of his first acts upon assuming the presidency of Cuba was to seize the magnificent private collection of Napoleonic letters formed by Señor Julio Lobo.

* *See key to abbreviations, p. 11.*

	SIG.	DS/LS	ALS	SP *
Konrad Adenauer	$7	$15	$25	$20
Spiro Agnew	5	10	25	10
Idi Amin	25	75	125	35
David R. Atchison	75	150	250	300
Otto von Bismarck	45	75	135	100
Leonid I. Brezhnev	25	100	250	125
John Brown	85	200	400	—
W. J. Bryan	5	15	25	25
Edmund Burke	65	110	300	—
Aaron Burr	40	90	150	—
John C. Calhoun	15	50	80	100
Fidel Castro	30	50	200	200
Salmon P. Chase	15	30	75	75
Cesar Chavez	8	15	40	15
Winston S. Churchill	100	225	400	215
Henry Clay	25	60	135	110
Oliver Cromwell	250	750	3200	—
Georges Danton	125	300	850	—
Jefferson Davis	40	110	275	100
Eugene V. Debs	15	30	60	75
Charles de Gaulle	75	140	300	150
Thomas E. Dewey	3	7	12	5
Porfirio Díaz	10	20	35	35
Stephen A. Douglas	25	75	150	120
Anthony Eden	5	10	20	15
Indira Gandhi	8	20	40	15
Mohandas K. Gandhi	80	165	300	210
John N. Garner	5	10	15	8
V. Giscard d'Estaing	5	15	20	15
W. E. Gladstone	5	15	20	25
Barry Goldwater	3	5	10	5
Andrei A. Gromyko	12	20	65	35
Dag Hammarskjöld	50	125	250	110
Warren Hastings	25	60	80	—
Hirohito	110	325	1000	350
Ho Chi Minh	150	350	1000	400
Hubert H. Humphrey	5	10	25	10
Agustín de Iturbide	75	200	375	—
Benito Juárez	55	160	300	210
Edward Kennedy	7	15	30	15
Robert F. Kennedy	15	50	110	75
Alexander Kerensky	35	55	200	85

	SIG.	DS/LS	ALS	SP *
Nikita S. Khrushchev	$75	$250	$850	$250
Mackenzie King	7	15	25	15
Henry A. Kissinger	5	15	30	15
Paul Krüger	10	25	35	35
Dalai Lama	8	20	35	15
V. I. Lenin	375	2000	3500	850
David Lloyd George	5	20	30	20
Huey P. Long	25	75	85	50
Mao Tse-tung	300	600	1000	475
Jean Paul Marat	175	375	850	—
K. Metternich	15	60	85	—
Walter Mondale	3	8	15	5
Ralph Nader	3	10	15	5
Jawaharlal Nehru	10	30	85	35
H. J. T. Palmerston	8	20	25	—
William Pitt, the Elder	35	85	175	—
William Pitt, the Younger	25	55	125	—
Grigori E. Rasputin	300	550	825	—
Ronald Reagan	3	8	25	5
Cardinal Richelieu	100	350	825	—
Maximilien Robespierre	175	300	2500	—
Nelson A. Rockefeller	3	7	25	5
Dean Rusk	3	5	10	5
William H. Seward	10	20	45	75
Alfred E. Smith	5	15	65	20
Joseph Stalin	1500	4000	10,000	2500
Edwin M. Stanton	15	55	100	75
Adlai E. Stevenson (d. 1914)	8	20	35	60
Adlai E. Stevenson (d. 1965)	5	10	15	8
Sun Yat-sen	100	240	450	250
Charles M. Talleyrand	25	80	110	—
Leon Trotsky	150	325	1000	325
Pierre Elliott Trudeau	10	25	35	15
W. M. "Boss" Tweed	25	40	75	65
George C. Wallace	3	5	15	5
Henry A. Wallace	5	15	35	15
Robert Walpole	20	55	175	—
Daniel Webster	12	40	75	75
Harold Wilson	5	15	20	10

6. [signature]

7. [signature]

8. *I have the honor to be your obdt* [signature: A. Burr]

9. *1881.* [signature]

10. [signature: J. C. Calhoun]

11. [signature: Winston S. Churchill]

12. [signature: Danton]

13. [signature: H. Clay]

14. *very truly your friend* [signature: S. A. Douglas]

15. [signature: Porfirio Díaz]

16. [signature: Gladstone]

17. *With good wishes yours truly* [signature: W. J. Bryan] *July 26 1923*

6. *Konrad Adenauer*

7. *Spiro T. Agnew*

8. *Aaron Burr*

9. *Otto von Bismarck*

10. *John C. Calhoun*

11. *Winston S. Churchill*

12. *Georges Danton*

13. *Henry Clay*

14. *Stephen A. Douglas*

15. *Porfirio Díaz*

16. *W. E. Gladstone*

17. *William Jennings Bryan*

18.

19.

18. *Edmund Burke*

19. *John Brown*

20. *Oliver Cromwell (as general)*

21. *Oliver Cromwell (as Lord Protector)*

22. *Oliver Cromwell (in old age)*

23. *Mohandas K. Gandhi*

24. *Charles de Gaulle*

25. *Hirohito*

26. *Nikita S. Khrushchev*

27. *Alexander Kerensky*

28. *K. Metternich*

29. *Nelson Rockefeller*

30. *Sun Yat-sen*

20.

23.

21.

24.

22.

25.

26.

27.

28.

29.

30.

31

32

33

34

35

36

37

38

39

40

41

31. Ho Chi Minh

32. Agustín de Iturbide

33. Robert F. Kennedy

34. Henry A. Kissinger

35. William Pitt, the Younger

36. Dag Hammarskjöld

37. Jawaharlal Nehru

38. H. J. T. Palmerston

39. Huey P. Long

40. V. I. Lenin

41. Grigori E. Rasputin (autograph note signed "Grigori")

42

43

44

45

46

47

48

49

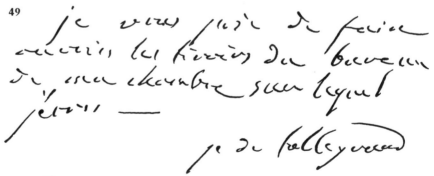

50

Composers

COMPOSERS ARE THE DARLINGS of autograph collectors, for their language is universal and their appeal has no geographical bounds. Eagerly sought but seldom found are the letters and documents of the early giants of music, such as Bach, Mozart and Beethoven. How exasperating to reflect, when we consider the enormous prices fetched by autographs of Beethoven, that the floor of his apartment was always littered with his original manuscripts, and he passed out these priceless relics lavishly to

1. *Johann Sebastian Bach (autograph note signed)*

2. *Wolfgang A. Mozart*

3. *Handwriting of Johannes Brahms*

casual visitors. You could have put your hand in Beethoven's wastebasket and drawn it out a rich man.

Beethoven's handwriting is a weird, almost illegible scrawl, but it is quite readable compared with the cryptograms that Brahms put into the mails. I once asked a well-educated German to translate a letter of Brahms. After an unsuccessful struggle, he turned the letter upside down and observed, ''Perhaps this will make it more legible.'' On another occasion, I was flooded with applicants for a job as a German translator and I tactfully weeded out those I didn't want by asking them to decode a letter of Brahms.

The great rarity of letters and manuscripts of the early masters is refreshingly relieved by the abundance of more recent composers. Even the most modest of collections may contain a little letter of Saint-Saëns or Massenet, and Leonard Bernstein once told me that he had signed his name so many times for signature seekers that there could not possibly be a collection lacking it.

A friend of mine was secretary to Gian Carlo Menotti many years ago when Menotti received the first mail request for his signature from an admirer. He gazed at the letter for a few minutes in pleasure and then asked, ''How shall I sign my name, modestly small or in big, bold script? And should I add a few bars of music?'' Today Menotti is blasé about such solicitations. He does not answer them.

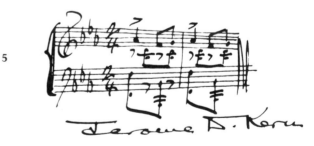

4. *Gian Carlo Menotti*

5. *Jerome Kern*

Jerome Kern was one of the most prominent rare book and autograph collectors of his generation, and his superb collection sold at auction in 1929 for $1 million, more than he had ever earned from his great songs. Another noted American composer, Jimmy Van Heusen, who owns more than a hundred hats, also is an avid philographer and prizes in his personal collection a rare complete manuscript of Irving Berlin's ''God Bless America.''

* See key to abbreviations, p. 11.

	SIG.	DS/LS	ALS	AQS	SP *
Leroy Anderson	$15	$35	$50	$65	$50
Harold Arlen	10	20	35	40	20
Johann Sebastian Bach	1500	8500	22,000	—	—
Burt Bacharach	20	30	35	40	25
Béla Bartók	85	185	300	425	200
Ludwig van Beethoven	1000	2750	4800	6000	—
Irving Berlin	15	35	100	250	25
Hector Berlioz	100	175	300	625	—
Leonard Bernstein	10	25	55	50	30
Georges Bizet	75	150	265	500	—
Eubie Blake	20	45	75	100	40
Alexander Borodin	100	250	550	750	—
Johannes Brahms	125	225	375	1500	600
William Byrd	275	1800	3200	—	—
Charles Wakefield Cadman	10	18	25	50	25
Hoagy Carmichael	15	25	60	40	20
Frédéric Chopin	500	900	1700	3900	—
George M. Cohan	35	55	75	300	—
Aaron Copland	20	50	65	90	—
Claude Debussy	85	130	175	550	375
Gaetano Donizetti	100	175	300	700	—
Antonin Dvořák	110	250	425	575	400
Gus Edwards	25	55	75	80	50
Duke Ellington	15	25	50	75	25
Daniel D. Emmett	150	250	300	650	—
Stephen Foster	600	2000	5500	—	—
César Franck	75	150	200	325	185
Rudolf Friml	45	65	85	225	85
George Gershwin	100	165	400	425	250
Christoph Gluck	450	850	2500	—	—
Charles Gounod	30	55	65	135	90
Edvard Grieg	60	80	125	285	125
George F. Handel	500	3500	13,000	—	—
W. C. Handy	30	60	150	150	55
Joseph Haydn	350	1000	2300	—	—
Victor Herbert	45	65	90	110	65
Charles Ives	25	60	125	250	100
Scott Joplin	400	1200	—	—	—
Jerome Kern	50	75	125	150	85
Aram Khachaturian	60	90	250	300	175
Fritz Kreisler	10	20	30	35	20
Franz Lehar	40	65	110	110	75

	SIG.	DS/LS	ALS	AQS	SP *
Ruggiero Leoncavallo	$40	$55	$65	$140	$75
Franz Liszt	75	150	300	525	275
Frederick Loewe	10	30	50	60	35
Edward MacDowell	40	80	120	150	150
Gustav Mahler	100	225	400	1200	500
Pietro Mascagni	35	90	110	125	60
Jules Massenet	20	50	65	110	75
Felix Mendelssohn	90	250	350	1250	—
Gian Carlo Menotti	65	150	250	250	150
Wolfgang Amadeus Mozart	1500	5000	18,500	—	—
Jacques Offenbach	40	75	85	175	100
I. J. Paderewski	25	45	90	85	70
Nicolò Paganini	110	250	525	850	—
Cole Porter	40	50	100	275	45
Sergei Prokofiev	100	175	450	175	150
Giacomo Puccini	60	100	135	300	135
Sergei Rachmaninoff	50	70	175	175	125
Maurice Ravel	85	150	275	425	235
N. Rimsky-Korsakov	125	310	450	650	325
Richard Rodgers	10	20	35	65	25
Sigmund Romberg	40	55	100	125	65
George F. Root	15	25	45	55	—
G. Rossini	60	125	250	450	300
Camille Saint-Saëns	35	75	110	225	100
Alessandro Scarlatti	400	2500	7000	—	—
Arnold Schœnberg	90	125	300	250	160
Franz Schubert	1000	3000	5000	—	—
Robert Schumann	250	575	750	1800	—
Dimitri Shostakovich	100	250	375	275	185
Jean Sibelius	50	90	175	275	150
John Philip Sousa	35	55	90	165	75
Johann Strauss (father)	50	85	100	125	—
Johann Strauss (son)	60	100	125	175	175
Richard Strauss	75	110	175	275	110
Igor Stravinsky	75	115	175	250	100
Arthur Sullivan	65	150	250	325	200
Peter Tchaikovsky	200	350	650	1100	750
Jimmy Van Heusen	10	20	35	35	20
Giuseppe Verdi	150	300	450	900	350
Richard Wagner	175	250	400	850	425
Thomas "Fats" Waller	15	20	40	55	20
Karl Maria von Weber	150	350	550	—	—
Kurt Weill	30	50	85	150	—
Hugo Wolf	200	375	550	1100	550

6. *Georges Bizet*

7. *Hector Berlioz*

8. *Alexander Borodin*

9. *Ludwig van Beethoven (autograph note signed)*

10. *Johannes Brahms (autograph music signed)*

11. *Ludwig van Beethoven (in German script)*

12. *William Byrd*

13. *Claude Debussy*

14. *Gaetano Donizetti*

15. *Frédéric Chopin*

16. *Hoagy Carmichael*

17. *Antonin Dvořák*

18. *Béla Bartók (autograph music signed)*

19. *Duke Ellington*

20. *George Gershwin (self-portrait)*

21. *Stephen Foster*

22. *Edvard Grieg*

23. *Christoph Gluck*

24

25

27

28

29

30

31

33

32

34

24. *Victor Herbert (autograph music signed)*

25. *George F. Handel*

26. *W. C. Handy*

27. *W. C. Handy (after blindness)*

28. *Franz Liszt*

29. *Franz Lehar*

30. *Joseph Haydn*

31. *Scott Joplin*

32. *Aram Khachaturian (autograph music signed)*

33. *Charles Ives*

34. *Pietro Mascagni (autograph music signed)*

35. *Jacques Offenbach*

36. *I. J. Paderewski*

37. *Felix Mendelssohn*

38. *Edward MacDowell (autograph music signed)*

39. *Nicolo Paganini*

40. *N. Rimsky-Korsakov (autograph music signed)*

41. *Giacomo Puccini (autograph music signed)*

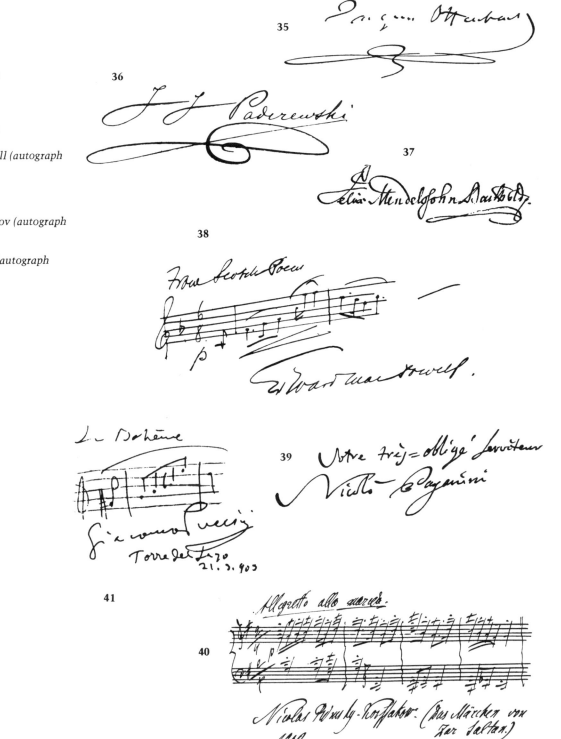

42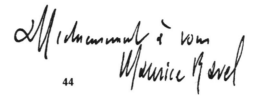

43

44

45

42. *Sergei Prokofiev*

43. *Cole Porter (autograph music signed)*

44. *Maurice Ravel*

45. *G. Rossini (autograph music signed)*

46. *Richard Rodgers*

47. *Robert Schumann*

48. *Franz Schubert (autograph letter signed)*

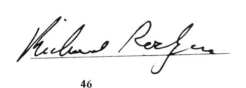

46

47

48

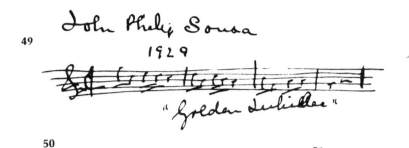

49. *John Philip Sousa (autograph music signed)*

50. *Richard Strauss (autograph music signed)*

51. *Johann Strauss (father)*

52. *Johann Strauss (son)*

53. *Jean Sibelius*

54. *Dimitri Shostakovich*

55. *Arnold Schœnberg*

56. *Camille Saint-Saëns (autograph music signed)*

57. *Igor Stravinsky*

58. *Peter Tchaikovsky*

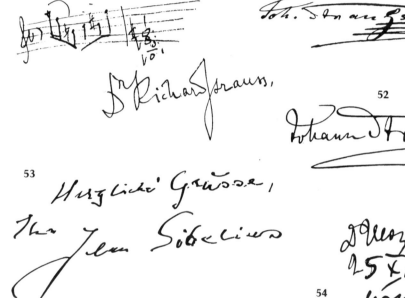

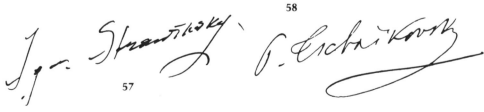

59

60

61

62

63

59. *Alessandro Scarlatti*

60. *Richard Wagner (autograph music signed)*

61. *Arthur Sullivan*

62. *Giuseppe Verdi*

63. *Carl Maria von Weber*

American Authors

As a boy of fourteen, I greatly admired Vachel Lindsay, whose poem "The Congo" I had committed to memory. I wrote to the famed poet five times asking for his signature but received no answer. Finally I made a last, desperate effort. "Forgive me for bothering you," I wrote. "I have just learned that your wife forbids you to send your autograph." By return mail I received a handsome signed photo.

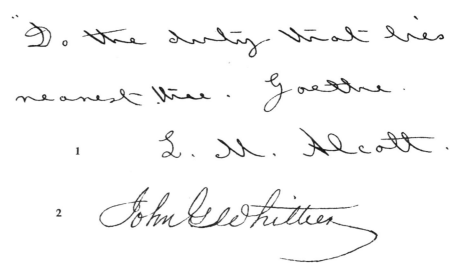

1. *Louisa May Alcott (autograph quotation signed)*

2. *John G. Whittier*

Many of the New England authors—Whittier, Bryant and Louisa May Alcott, for example—frequently wrote their missives in purple ink. This ink, of analine dye and unlike the earlier iron gall ink, runs when wet and fades rapidly in bright light. Years ago I placed in the window of my gallery, where the sun could reveal its attractiveness, a framed sonnet written out and signed by Bryant. About three weeks later someone wryly asked why I had framed a blank piece of paper. I looked and found the Bryant sonnet had completely vanished in the sun's rays.

Mark Twain always good-naturedly complied with requests for his "autograph and a sentiment," but his amiability once buckled under the strain. "No man takes pleasure in exercising his trade as a pastime," he wrote. "It would never be fair to ask a doctor for one of his corpses to remember him by."

Edgar Allan Poe, whose autograph is the most valuable of any major

American author, was himself an avid philographer. He wrote a lengthy series of articles on "autography," in which he proved himself, long before the science developed, a skilled graphoanalyst.

Fashion sets the value for literary autographs, and the critics tell us what the fashion is. Take a look through the catalogues of old-time autograph dealers and you will find letters of Bayard Taylor, now almost forgotten, at $50 and $75, and letters of Walt Whitman, now in favor with critics but then ignored, at $5 or $10. Herman Melville sold for only a dollar or two. Fame did not come to him until thirty years after his death in 1891.

3. *Mark Twain (S. L. Clemens)*
(autograph quotation signed)

4. *Bayard Taylor (autograph quotation signed)*

4

The bravest are the tenderest,
The loving are the daring.

Bayard Taylor.

The moral is clear. Don't be stampeded by the critics. Collect what interests you. And, who knows, if your taste is impeccable and your luck has a touch of Erin, you may acquire a fortune in literary letters for the proverbial aria.

* See key to abbreviations, p. 11.

	SIG.	DS/LS	ALS *
Henry Adams	$35	$75	$225
Conrad Aiken	15	35	85
Louisa May Alcott	30	75	150
Horatio Alger	20	40	75
Sherwood Anderson	10	30	50
W. H. Auden	25	45	125
L. Frank Baum	40	85	175
Robert Benchley	10	30	50
Ambrose Bierce	50	125	300
Anne Bradstreet	250	750	1500
William Cullen Bryant	10	20	40
Pearl Buck	5	15	35
Edgar Rice Burroughs	20	35	75
Truman Capote	20	60	150
Willa Cather	25	75	175
Paddy Chayefsky	15	35	65
Samuel L. Clemens	55	125	250
James Fenimore Cooper	25	50	150
Hart Crane	85	400	1000
Stephen Crane	100	350	800
E. E. Cummings	45	75	125
John Dewey	20	50	90
Emily Dickinson	225	—	2000
Theodore Dreiser	15	30	75
T. S. Eliot	35	100	450

	SIG.	DS/LS	ALS *
Ralph Waldo Emerson	$ 35	$ 50	$ 150
William Faulkner	75	500	1000
Eugene Field	35	35	75
F. Scott Fitzgerald	75	350	650
Philip Freneau	100	350	850
Robert Frost	60	100	450
Allen Ginsberg	15	25	50
Horace Greeley	10	35	50
Zane Grey	5	25	75
Edgar A. Guest	3	10	10
Dashiell Hammett	5	20	35
Bret Harte	20	60	85
Nathaniel Hawthorne	50	100	600
Lafcadio Hearn	85	225	500
Ernest Hemingway	75	350	500
Oliver Wendell Holmes, Sr.	10	35	50
Julia Ward Howe	10	25	30
Washington Irving	25	75	125
Henry James	30	85	160
Randall Jarrell	25	50	80
Robinson Jeffers	25	60	150
James Jones	15	35	85
Jack Kerouac	15	50	80
Francis Scott Key	50	125	150
Joyce Kilmer	25	50	75
Sidney Lanier	75	200	375
Stephen Leacock (Canada)	7	20	35
Sinclair Lewis	15	40	125
Vachel Lindsay	15	35	85
Jack London	40	100	250
Henry W. Longfellow	10	45	75
James Russell Lowell	10	25	50
Rod McKuen	5	15	20
Norman Mailer	10	35	100
John P. Marquand	10	25	65
Edgar Lee Masters	10	25	50
Herman Melville	225	500	1500
H. L. Mencken	5	15	30
Edna St. Vincent Millay	50	150	350
Henry Miller	15	30	40
Margaret Mitchell	35	60	125
Marianne Moore	15	30	70
Christopher Morley	10	35	65
Ogden Nash	3	10	12

	SIG.	DS/LS	ALS *
Frank Norris	$80	$175	$400
Eugene O'Neill	60	125	400
Thomas Paine	300	700	2000
Edgar Allan Poe	750	1200	3500
William Sydney Porter (O. Henry)	175	350	700
Ezra Pound	40	175	250
James Whitcomb Riley	12	35	65
E. A. Robinson	15	35	70
J. D. Salinger	40	150	250
Carl Sandburg	15	35	100
William Saroyan	10	30	80
Upton Sinclair	5	15	35
Samuel Francis Smith	10	30	50
Mickey Spillane	8	10	15
Gertrude Stein	35	100	350
John Steinbeck	30	100	300
Wallace Stevens	25	75	200
Harriet Beecher Stowe	25	75	125
Booth Tarkington	10	35	55
Henry David Thoreau	200	500	1500
Gore Vidal	8	20	35
Walt Whitman	150	300	1000
John Greenleaf Whittier	10	40	60
Thornton Wilder	15	40	80
William Carlos Williams	20	90	200
Thomas Wolfe	100	350	700
Herman Wouk	5	20	35

5. *Henry Adams*

6. *William Cullen Bryant*

7. *Anne Bradstreet*

5

6

7

8

10

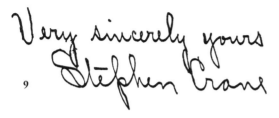
9

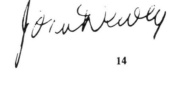
11

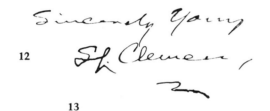
12

13

14

16

15

17

18

20

19

21

8. *Paddy Chayefsky*

9. *Stephen Crane*

10. *Hart Crane*

11. *E. E. Cummings*

12. *S. L. Clemens (Mark Twain)*

13. *James Fenimore Cooper*

14. *John Dewey*

15. *Emily Dickinson*

16. *T. S. Eliot*

17. *Eugene Field*

18. *Philip Freneau*

19. *Allen Ginsberg*

20. *Bret Harte*

21. *Horace Greeley*

22. *Julia Ward Howe (autograph quotation signed)*

23. *Ernest Hemingway*

24. *Francis Scott Key*

25. *Washington Irving*

26. *James Jones*

27. *Henry James*

28. *Robinson Jeffers*

29. *Randall Jarrell*

30. *Jack Kerouac*

31. *Henry W. Longfellow*

32. *Jack London*

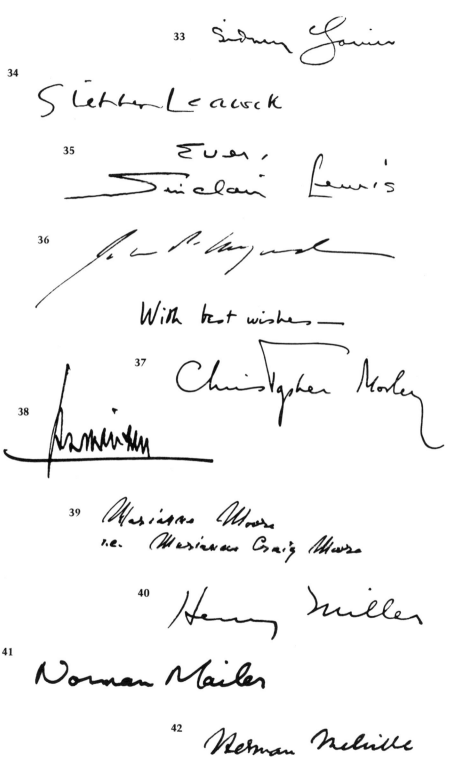

33. *Sidney Lanier*

34. *Stephen Leacock (Canada)*

35. *Sinclair Lewis*

36. *John P. Marquand*

37. *Christopher Morley*

38. *H. L. Mencken*

39. *Marianne Moore*

40. *Henry Miller*

41. *Norman Mailer*

42. *Herman Melville*

43

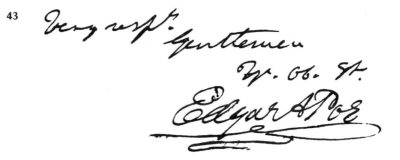

44

45

46

47

48

49  *Thomas Paine*

50 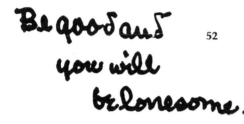 *J. D. Salinger*

51 *Gertrude Stein*

52 *Carl Sandburg (autograph quotation signed)*

Be good and you will be lonesome.

53 Yours very truly, Wallace Stevens

Carl Sandburg

54

55 Henry D. Thoreau

56 Very truly Yours Mark Twain

57 Sincerely Thornton Wilder

58 Tom Wolfe

59 Walt Whitman

49. *Thomas Paine*

50. *J. D. Salinger*

51. *Gertrude Stein*

52. *Carl Sandburg (autograph quotation signed)*

53. *Wallace Stevens*

54. *Harriet Beecher Stowe*

55. *Henry David Thoreau*

56. *Mark Twain*

57. *Thornton Wilder*

58. *Thomas Wolfe*

59. *Walt Whitman*

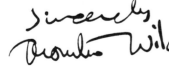

Entertainment Personalities of the Present

MANY YEARS AGO I was lunching with my then wife, Doris Harris, and a friend, Bob Black, and we spotted Buster Crabbe at a nearby table. Doris is remotely related to Buster and I had met him many times. Buster joined us at our table and we introduced him to Mr. Black. For about half an hour we chatted, and when he left, Bob Black observed, "Funny, isn't it? He not only has the same name as Buster Crabbe but he even looks like him."

When we told Bob it really was Buster Crabbe, he exclaimed, "Gosh! I should have asked for his autograph."

The bullish market in movie actors' autographs will remind many collectors that they should have asked for, or collected, such autographs years ago.

The upward surge of prices for movie star autographs brings to mind a recent auction at which, among several hundred other items, I offered a rare signed photograph of Greta Garbo, well known for her Olympian

1. *Greta Garbo*

1   *Greta Garbo*

disdain of signature seekers. Her signed photo was the first item in the sale, a notoriously poor spot, since many collectors arrive late. Ignorant of the increased interest in movie stars of the age of nostalgia, I had estimated its value at $75.

I was amazed when the bidding opened at $190. By jumps of $25, the bidding mounted rapidly before an excited crowd until it reached $500.

There were murmurs of incredulity in the audience. I said to myself, Someone has made an error and will now retract his bid.

"I have $525," cried the auctioneer.

On went the bidding, and when the photo was finally knocked down to a dealer for $675—a new world's record for a signed photo of a movie star—I stepped out of the auction room for a breath of air. Since then, her autograph has risen in value.

Should you be inspired to seek a Garbo signature in person, be forewarned that she carries a heavy handbag (some say it is weighted with stones) which she wields mightily and effectively when approached by signature hunters.

Among noted film stars, Glenn Ford and Hugh O'Brian are enthusiastic philographers.

* See key to abbreviations, p. 11.

	SIG.	DS/LS	ALS	AQS	SP *
Jack Albertson	$3	$10	$15	$10	$10
Woody Allen	3	10	15	10	10
Fred Astaire	6	12	20	15	15
Robert Blake	6	12	20	15	15
Ray Bolger	6	12	20	15	20
Marlon Brando	8	15	25	15	20
Charles Bronson	6	12	20	15	15
George Burns	6	10	20	10	15
Richard Burton	8	15	25	15	20
James Cagney	10	15	25	15	25
Johnny Carson	3	10	15	10	10
Dick Cavett	3	10	15	10	10
Jackie Coogan	8	12	20	10	15
Joseph Cotten	8	12	20	10	15
Buster Crabbe	5	10	15	10	10
Bette Davis	10	20	40	20	20
Sammy Davis, Jr.	6	12	20	15	15
Olivia de Havilland	8	12	25	12	15
Marlene Dietrich	8	15	25	15	15
Kirk Douglas	3	10	15	10	10
Jimmy Durante	8	15	25	15	20
Henry Fonda	3	10	15	10	10
Jane Fonda	6	12	20	15	15
Joan Fontaine	8	12	25	12	15
Lynn Fontanne	10	20	25	10	15
Greta Garbo	200	400	750	350	750
Frank Gifford	5	10	15	10	10
Jackie Gleason	6	12	15	8	10
Benny Goodman	6	12	20	15	15
Elliott Gould	6	12	20	15	15
Cary Grant	10	15	25	20	20
Alec Guinness	10	15	25	20	20
Helen Hayes	10	15	30	15	15
Katharine Hepburn	10	15	25	20	20

	SIG.	DS/LS	ALS	AQS	SP *
Alfred Hitchcock	$8	$15	$25	$15	$20
Dustin Hoffman	6	12	20	15	15
William Holden	3	10	15	10	10
Bob Hope	8	15	25	15	20
Jack Jones	3	10	15	10	10
Emmett Kelly	6	12	20	15	15
Grace Kelly	6	12	20	15	20
Burt Lancaster	8	15	25	15	20
Jack Lemmon	6	12	20	15	15
Mantovani	6	12	20	15	10
Dean Martin	3	10	15	10	10
Lee Marvin	6	12	15	15	15
Raymond Massey	10	15	25	15	20
Johnny Mathis	6	12	20	15	10
Walter Matthau	6	12	20	15	15
Yehudi Menuhin	8	15	25	15	20
Liza Minnelli	6	12	15	15	20
Paul Newman	10	15	25	15	35
Jack Nicholson	6	12	20	15	15
Rudolf Nureyev	8	15	25	15	25
Donald O'Connor	10	15	25	12	15
Laurence Olivier	10	15	25	15	20
Ryan O'Neal	6	12	15	15	15
Peter O'Toole	6	12	20	15	15
Gregory Peck	6	12	20	15	15
Walter Pidgeon	6	10	15	10	15
Roman Polanski	8	15	25	15	25
William Powell	10	15	30	15	20
Vincent Price	8	15	25	15	20
Robert Redford	6	12	20	15	20
Burt Reynolds	5	10	15	10	15
Mickey Rooney	6	12	20	15	15
Telly Savalas	6	12	20	15	15
George C. Scott	8	15	20	15	15
George Segal	6	12	20	15	15
Frank Sinatra	10	20	35	20	25
Jimmy Stewart	8	15	25	15	15
Barbra Streisand	10	20	35	20	30
Gloria Swanson	10	20	35	20	25
Elizabeth Taylor	15	25	50	25	35
Shirley Temple	6	12	15	8	10
Richard Widmark	8	15	20	12	15
Fay Wray	10	20	35	20	40
Darryl F. Zanuck	8	15	25	15	15

2

3

4

2. *George Burns*

3. *Johnny Carson*

4. *Joseph Cotten*

5. *Jackie Coogan*

6. *Bob Hope*

7. *Dean Martin and Jerry Lewis*

5

6

7

8

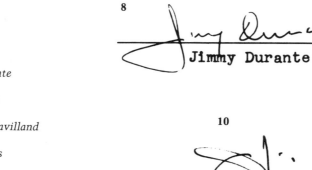

Jimmy Durante

9

10

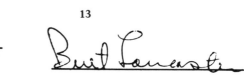

11

12

13

14

15

16

17

18

19

20

21

22

23

24   193 9

25

18. *Walter Pidgeon*

19. *William Powell*

20. *Frank Sinatra*

21. *Vincent Price*

22. *Gloria Swanson*

23. *Jimmy Stewart*

24. *Shirley Temple*

25. *Richard Widmark*

Artists
and
Photographers

THE MOST FLAMBOYANT SIGNATURES and the most delightful letters come from the artists. Maxfield Parrish sometimes fills half a page with his graceful, cursive capital *P*. Howard Pyle often adds a pirate sketch to his name, Whistler a butterfly, Remington a bucking bronco, and Charles M. Russell a steer's skull. So well known are these trademarks that they have attracted forgers. I've seen enough spurious Remington broncos to stock a rodeo.

Many of the great artists—Renoir and Van Gogh, for example—adorned their letters with sketches. Such epistles are highly prized by philographers and fetch great prices in the auction room.

No artist was ever more eccentric than Dali, who is often pursued by

1. *Maxfield Parrish*

2. *Howard Pyle (autograph sketch signed)*

74

My Book

Frederic Remington

3

Your faithful

Frederic Remington

4

5

une manuscrite adresse, dites moi

si vous avez revu elle si

si vous vouler venir voir le petit Dri

Bonjour Drapeau !

3. *Forgery of a sketch by Frederic Remington*

4. *Frederic Remington (authentic)*

5. *Salvador Dali (autograph note signed)*

signature hunters in the dining room of the St. Regis hotel in New York. Dali usually obliges, often adding a sketch, but always pockets the collector's pen. A friend of mine watched his favorite gold pen disappear into Dali's coat. When he asked the artist to return it, Dali hurled it at him in a fit of pique.

A final caution to collectors of artists: If you run across an ancient piece of paper with a list of numerals on it, don't throw it away. It may be a portrait sketch by Da Vinci. The famed artist used to make preliminary portraits of people he saw in the street by giving each facial feature a number: a 21 nose, 60 mouth, 26 lip, 18 chin, and so on, so that he could construct a complete face later in the privacy of his studio.

* *See key to abbreviations, p. 11.*

	SIG.	DS/LS	ALS *
John J. Audubon	$125	$325	$800
Aubrey Beardsley	75	150	225
George Bellows	35	80	135
Thomas Hart Benton	15	30	60
Albert Bierstadt	20	50	75
Rosa Bonheur	20	35	50
Margaret Bourke-White	20	35	80
Mathew B. Brady	75	300	750
Georges Braque	50	160	260
Alexander Calder	10	20	50
Al Capp	5	12	20
Benvenuto Cellini	350	1800	4500
Paul Cézanne	200	500	1800
Marc Chagall	25	75	150
John Singleton Copley	100	225	450
J. B. C. Corot	45	75	90
Gustave Courbet	75	150	300
George Cruikshank	25	45	55
Salvador Dali	15	25	100
Honoré Daumier	75	225	375
Jacques Louis David	55	125	250
Jo Davidson	12	20	30
Edgar Degas	65	125	200
Eugène Delacroix	35	65	80
Walt Disney	100	160	375
Albrecht Dürer	1500	4000	13,000
James Montgomery Flagg	5	20	40
Daniel Chester French	10	20	30
Thomas Gainsborough	75	225	350
Paul Gauguin	170	350	750
Charles Dana Gibson	5	20	35
Vincent van Gogh	750	3000	8000
Rube Goldberg	8	15	30
Francisco Goya	500	2500	6000
Childe Hassam	15	45	60
William Hogarth	150	450	1000
Winslow Homer	80	150	375
Will James	20	50	85
Wassily Kandinsky	50	110	200
Rockwell Kent	10	20	35
John Leech	20	40	55
Aristide Maillol	60	135	200

	SIG.	DS/LS	ALS *
Édouard Manet	$75	$210	$300
Henri Matisse	30	55	125
Michelangelo Buonarroti	1000	6000	15,000
J. F. Millet	35	65	110
A. Modigliani	100	350	900
Claude Monet	60	85	175
Grandma Moses	15	25	55
Nadar	30	80	150
Thomas Nast	12	25	35
Maxfield Parrish	15	60	100
Charles Willson Peale	75	185	325
Pablo Picasso	75	160	400
Camille Pissarro	50	110	175
Howard Pyle	20	50	100
Arthur Rackham	25	60	110
Raphael	900	3500	13,000
Rembrandt van Rijn	1500	8000	25,000
Frederic Remington	110	185	275
Pierre Auguste Renoir	50	110	165
Joshua Reynolds	70	175	275
Diego Rivera	45	85	175
Norman Rockwell	5	10	20
Auguste Rodin	20	35	50
Dante Gabriel Rossetti	30	85	100
Georges Rouault	50	125	350
Thomas Rowlandson	85	300	500
Charles M. Russell	100	300	650
Albert Pinkham Ryder	25	80	160
Augustus Saint-Gaudens	15	20	35
John Singer Sargent	15	30	50
Charles M. Schulz	5	15	30
Ben Shahn	10	25	35
Paul Signac	40	90	150
Edward Steichen	25	45	70
Alfred Stieglitz	25	55	75
Gilbert Stuart	100	400	700
James Thurber	30	85	150
Louis C. Tiffany	25	75	85
Titian	500	1500	3000
Henri de Toulouse-Lautrec	65	200	350
J. M. W. Turner	35	75	110
John Trumbull	30	85	110
Maurice Utrillo	75	225	375
Leonardo da Vinci	3000	8000	20,000

	SIG.	DS/LS	ALS *
Maurice de Vlaminck	$ 45	$ 100	$ 200
Andy Warhol	10	25	35
Benjamin West	25	80	160
James A. McNeill Whistler	35	65	110
Andrew Wyeth	15	60	130
N. C. Wyeth	25	80	160

6. *John J. Audubon*

7. *Aubrey Beardsley*

8. *Thomas Hart Benton (autograph sketch signed)*

9. *Mathew Brady*

10. *Edgar Degas*

11. *Paul Cézanne (autograph note signed)*

12

13

14

15

16

17

18

19

20

12. *Marc Chagall*

13. *Gustave Courbet*

14. *Walt Disney*

15. *Eugène Delacroix*

16. *Honoré Daumier*

17. *Jacques Louis David*

18. *Francisco Goya*

19. *Thomas Gainsborough*

20. *Rube Goldberg*

21. *Childe Hassam*

22. *Paul Gauguin*

23. *Winslow Homer*

24. *Wassily Kandinsky*

25. *Eadweard Muybridge*

26. *Henri de Toulouse-Lautrec*

27. *Grandma Moses*

21

22

23

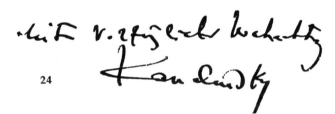

24

25

26

27

29

Th: Nast.
April 5.
1883

28

aristide Maillol

30

Vostro Anto lagmolo Schultore in Firenzo

31

Claude Monet

32

Henri : Matisse

33

34

Ed. Manet

35

C. Pissarro.

Jo raphaello

37

Sincerely,

Diego Rivera

36

28. *Aristide Maillol*

29. *Thomas Nast (self-portrait)*

30. *Michelangelo*

31. *Claude Monet*

32. *Henri Matisse*

33. *Arthur Rackham (autograph sketch signed)*

34. *Édouard Manet*

35. *Camille Pissarro*

36. *Raphael*

37. *Diego Rivera*

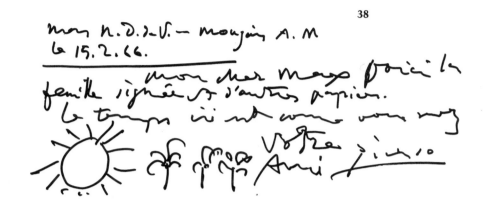

47

[autograph note in French]

48

49

51

50

52

53

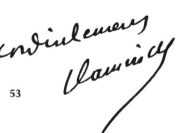

54

55

Very truly yours,

Edward Steichen

47. *Pierre Auguste Renoir (autograph note signed)*

48. *John Trumbull*

49. *Benjamin West*

50. *James Thurber*

51. *Leonardo da Vinci*

52. *John Singer Sargent*

53. *Maurice de Vlaminck*

54. *Vincent van Gogh*

55. *Edward Steichen*

Whimsical Signatures

1. *Thomas Hood, English poet*

2. *Earl Wilson, columnist*

3. *Wilhelm von Kaulbach, German artist*

4. *Germain Pillon, French sculptor*

5

5. *Benjamin Robert Haydon, English artist*

6. *Liberace, American pianist*

7. *Sir John Betjeman, English poet laureate*

8. *Ezra Pound, American poet*

These flamboyant signatures capture the exuberance of the writers. They are considered very desirable by collectors and fetch much more than routine examples by the same persons.

6

8

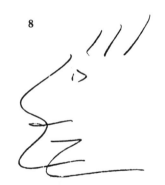

7

Colonial and Revolutionary Leaders

MANY OF THE MOST dramatic letters of early Americans were penned in ink made from gunpowder, a light gray flecked with black specks. Such letters often tell of Indian fights and scalping raids and frontier battles. They are the raw stuff of history.

As might be expected, the autographs of Colonial leaders are rare and command high prices whenever they appear on the market. I once met a rather distinguished looking man who smugly told me, "I recently

1. *William Penn (autograph note signed)*

bought an old house in Pennsylvania, fully furnished, for $15,000, and in a desk in the library I discovered a whole bundle of letters of William Penn. They seemed to have little or no value so I burned them."

"From a financial point of view," I said, "you would have done better to burn the house and keep the letters." The man's smug look vanished and his face turned so ashen that for a moment I thought he was going to faint.

If you happen to be well heeled, I recommend that you form a collection of important letters and documents of Revolutionary War leaders. Such an assemblage can only grow in value and, as its historic worth increases, it may become a mecca for scholars.

* See key to abbreviations, p. 11.

	SIG.	DS/LS	ALS *
John Alden	$750	$2700	$3500
Ethan Allen	350	850	3500
Jeffrey Amherst	85	210	325
John André	350	950	2000
Edmund Andros	150	300	500
Benedict Arnold	250	550	1000
Jonathan Belcher	100	185	275
Edward Braddock	250	700	1600
William Bradford	175	550	1750
John Burgoyne	175	350	825
George Rogers Clark	400	1800	4500
George Clinton	50	135	425
Henry Clinton	60	150	200
Charles, Lord Cornwallis	85	160	225
Comte de Frontenac	225	1200	2750
Horatio Gates	85	250	575
Nathanael Greene	80	275	750
Nathan Hale	4500	15,000	25,000
Patrick Henry	225	325	1000
Thomas Hutchinson	50	125	350
John Paul Jones	800	1800	3500
Johann de Kalb	150	875	1800
Henry Knox	50	150	265
Thaddeus Kosciusko	75	185	375
Marquis de Lafayette	50	110	225
Charles Lee	75	250	450
Light-Horse Harry Lee	50	150	250
Benjamin Lincoln	40	110	250
Francis Marion	225	475	1500
Peter Minuit	1200	3500	7500
Daniel Morgan	85	225	450
James Oglethorpe	500	1800	2200
James Otis	65	175	225
John Parker	175	450	1800
William Penn	250	650	1500
William Pepperell	65	165	275
Timothy Pickering	35	100	175
William Prescott	75	225	375
Casimir Pulaski	450	3000	5000
Israel Putnam	200	825	2300
Rufus Putnam	85	250	600
Walter Raleigh	1200	3200	6500

	SIG.	DS/LS	ALS *
Paul Revere	$ 350	$ 850	$ 2000
Comte de Rochambeau	110	200	350
Robert Rogers	225	800	2200
Arthur St. Clair	100	225	450
Philip Schuyler	65	125	225
Samuel Sewall	65	225	650
William Shirley	45	125	375
John Smith	1500	7500	20,000
Myles Standish	1200	6000	18,000
John Stark	175	275	650
Baron von Steuben	100	185	850
Peter Stuyvesant	800	2800	12,000
John Sullivan	50	150	275
Anthony Wayne	100	185	575
James Wilkinson	60	·135	200
John Winthrop	500	1250	3000

2

2. *Benedict Arnold (pass for John André dated only hours before Arnold's treason was discovered)*

3. *Ethan Allen (autograph note signed)*

4 *Your most obedient*
and most humble Servant

John André

5 *Jeff Amherst*   6 *E Braddock*

7 *Camp Saratoga oct, 15 1777*

J. Burgoyne   *Horatio Gates*

Saratoga
Octbr 17. 1777

9

8

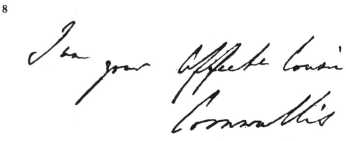

Cornwallis

10 *Frontenac*   11 *P. Henry*

4. *John André*

5. *Jeffrey Amherst*

6. *Edward Braddock*

7. *John Burgoyne and Horatio Gates*
(signatures on Burgoyne's surrender)

8. *Cornwallis*

9. *George Rogers Clark*

10. *Louis de Frontenac*

11. *Patrick Henry*

20

21

22

23

24 Samuel Sewall.

25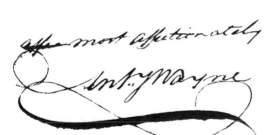

26

27

28

29 **30**

20. *Israel Putnam*

21. *Rufus Putnam*

22. *William Pepperell*

23. *John Sullivan*

24. *Samuel Sewall*

25. *Arthur St. Clair*

26. *Myles Standish*

27. *Anthony Wayne*

28. *John Winthrop (autograph note signed)*

29. *John Stark*

30. *William Shirley*

Explorers, Inventors, Airmen, and Architects

FEW AUTOGRAPHS ARE MORE colorful and dramatic than those of the great adventurers, the explorers who opened up the American continent, but scarcely any documents exist from the golden age of exploration. No amount of money can summon up what is not for sale or what does not exist.

On the other hand, of nineteenth-century explorers there is no dearth and I cordially commend to the collector an assemblage of African or

1. *Amerigo Vespucci*

2. *Ferdinand Magellan*

3. *Juan Ponce de León*

4. *Hernando de Soto*

Arctic explorers. They will never be cheaper than today and will continue to grow in value.

The early airmen and astronauts are extremely popular with seekers of

5. *The seven original astronauts: Alan B. Shepard, Jr.; Walter M. Schirra, Jr.; John H. Glenn, Jr.; Virgil I. Grissom; M. Scott Carpenter; Donald K. Slayton; and Leroy Gordon Cooper, Jr. With the exception of Grissom, who died in an accident and whose autographs are worth about three or four times as much as the others, these airmen fetch from about $5 to $10 for a signature to $75 to $100 for an autograph letter signed.*

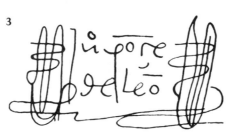

historic excitement. No autograph conveys more drama than the rare signature of Baron von Richthofen, the Red Knight, who shot down eighty planes before he died in aerial combat. On his last morning, just as

6

6. *Baron Manfred von Richthofen*

he was getting into his crimson Tri-Fokker, a young girl ran up to him and asked him to sign a photograph. It was considered unlucky to sign anything before takeoff, but Richthofen complied, smiled, and spoke his last words: "What's the hurry? Are you afraid I won't come back?"

* See key to abbreviations, p. 11.

	SIG.	DS/LS	ALS *
Buzz Aldrin	$5	$10	$100
Roald Amundsen	15	30	50
Neil Armstrong	5	12	200
Alexander Graham Bell	30	50	250
Frank Borman	5	10	100
Wernher von Braun	5	20	45
Sir Richard Burton	30	125	175
Richard E. Byrd	5	15	30
Samuel de Champlain	650	2800	9000
Samuel Colt	75	200	475
Christopher Columbus	—	—	150,000
Frederick A. Cook	15	40	65
Capt. James Cook	350	1700	3500
Glenn H. Curtis	35	75	135
Louis Daguerre	90	300	850
Hernando de Soto	—	15,000	25,000
James H. Doolittle	5	12	45
Sir Francis Drake	800	4000	12,500
Amelia Earhart	45	85	150
George Eastman	25	75	200
Thomas A. Edison	30	100	350
John Ericsson	25	85	110
Cyrus W. Field	5	25	35
John Fitch	125	300	650
Sir John Franklin	50	125	225
Robert Fulton	80	300	900
Yuri Gagarin	25	50	250
Richard J. Gatling	15	65	75

	SIG.	DS/LS	ALS *
John H. Glenn, Jr.	$ 5	$12	$ 85
Robert H. Goddard	60	225	425
George W. Goethals	10	20	65
Charles Goodyear	60	130	300
Elias Howe	65	160	350
Simon Lake	25	60	120
Samuel P. Langley	45	85	210
Charles Lindbergh	75	175	450
David Livingstone	75	150	175
Cyrus McCormick	45	125	275
Ferdinand Magellan	—	40,000	75,000
Gugielmo Marconi	40	75	150
Sir Hiram S. Maxim	25	65	125
Hudson Maxim	15	40	85
Billy Mitchell	40	100	225
Samuel F. B. Morse	40	85	150
Eadweard Muybridge	50	200	300
Alfred Nobel	75	150	225
Robert E. Peary	10	25	35
Ponce de León	—	15,000	25,000
Wiley Post	20	40	60
George M. Pullman	35	45	85
Baron Manfred von Richthofen	325	1000	2500
Capt. Eddie Rickenbacker	5	10	25
John A. Roebling	50	85	175
Washington A. Roebling	35	75	150
Wilhelm Roentgen	120	625	900
Sir John Ross	45	200	300
Igor Sikorsky	10	25	60
John H. Speke	30	100	250
Sir Henry M. Stanley	15	35	60
William Henry Fox Talbot	70	210	325
Amerigo Vespucci	—	—	60,000
James Watt	85	250	375
Stanford White	25	45	75
Eli Whitney	75	185	350
Christopher Wren	100	450	800
Frank Lloyd Wright	50	120	300
Orville Wright	35	150	350
Wilbur Wright	110	300	850
Count Ferdinand von Zeppelin	40	90	135

7

9

8

Apollo 11

10

11

12 Sincerely yours,

13

14

7. *Roald Amundsen*

8. *Buzz Aldrin and Neil Armstrong*

9. *Louis Daguerre*

10. *Francis Drake*

11. *Cyrus W. Field*

12. *Wernher von Braun*

13. *Alexander Graham Bell*

14. *Sir Richard F. Burton*

15. *Thomas A. Edison (autograph note signed)*

16. *Amelia Earhart*

17. *Richard E. Byrd*

18. *John Ericsson*

19. *Samuel Colt*

15 *Electricity will eventually furnish power for the world*

Thomas A. Edison.

16

17

Sincerely Yours,

19

18

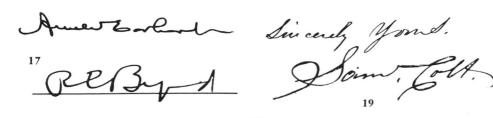

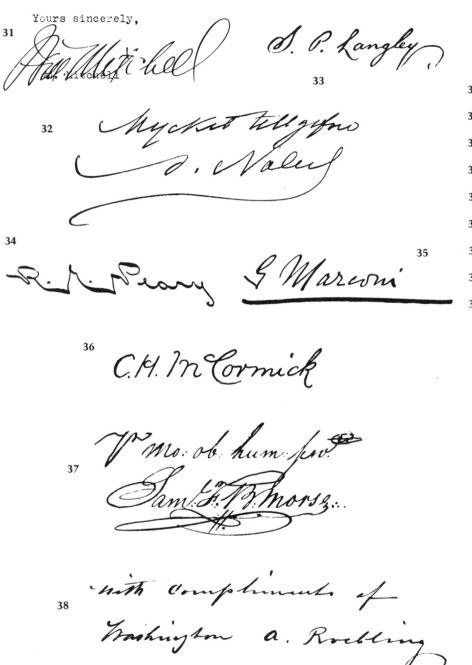

Yours sincerely,

31

32

33 S. P. Langley

34

35 G Marconi

36 C.H. McCormick

37

38 with compliments of Washington a. Roebling

39 yours truely

31. *Billy Mitchell*

32. *Alfred Nobel*

33. *Samuel P. Langley*

34. *Robert E. Peary*

35. *Gugielmo Marconi*

36. *Cyrus H. McCormick*

37. *Samuel F. B. Morse*

38. *Washington A. Roebling*

39. *Sir John Ross*

Famous
Women

"The Lord put women on earth to tempt us," wrote George Washington to a lady friend. Certainly Martha tempted George, for she occasionally lured him into acting as her private secretary. Martha's handwriting was crabbed and hard to read and she had trouble with spelling, so George helped her out. A letter penned by George and signed by Martha would be the gem of any collection of first ladies.

1

1. *Martha Washington*

Many collectors specialize in first ladies but I have never heard of a complete "set." Some, such as Martha Jefferson, Hannah Van Buren, and Margaret Taylor, are horrendously scarce and turn up only once in two or three generations. At a recent auction, one collector was so astonished at the high prices of first ladies that he exclaimed, "You'd think they were presidents!"

Still, many of the first ladies are, autographically speaking, refreshingly abundant. There is no dearth of letters of Eleanor Roosevelt or Patricia Nixon or Lady Bird Johnson. Jackie Onassis' letters are not rare but are highly prized. Ten years ago at one of my auction sales a letter of Jackie to a begging stranger in England was knocked down for $3000, the top price ever paid for a letter of a living person, now in the Guinness Book of World Records.

Jackie Onassis' letters are dynamite to sell at auction. Every time I have put one of this remarkable woman's letters on the block it has been a traumatic experience for me. I've had cops and the Secret Service huffing and puffing down my neck. I've been bombarded with "hate" mail, accusing me of a shameless invasion of the Great Lady's privacy and of mortgaging my soul for sordid gain. Yet I cannot resist Jackie's letters. They are my undoing, but I am driven by a fierce compulsion to handle them, for they fascinate me.

Jackie is the world's greatest living letter writer. Her dainty missives, indited in a delicate cursive script, are *intime* and persuasive, beautifully phrased, full of the excitement of the woman herself. She lays bare her psyche even when writing to strangers. I foresee the day, not far distant, when her letters will be gathered into a volume which will instantly become a classic. College students two hundred years from now will study her letters as models of the epistolary art.

I recall a little incident about Jackie that never got into the papers. One afternoon about two years ago two excited young men burst into my gallery. "Can you identify Jackie Onassis' signature?" they asked.

"Certainly."

"Well, we published in our current issue of *Hustler,* in full color, some nude photos of Jackie, and a man just phoned and said he had one of our magazines in which Jackie had personally signed a nude photo. If so, it's very valuable to us. We asked him to meet us here."

It seemed very unlikely, I thought, that Jackie would put her signature on such a revealing portrait.

A few minutes later the signature owner showed up, triumphantly waving a copy of *Hustler.* "Signed in person!" he exclaimed, as he opened a page to show me.

The signature was not Jackie's. "This is the most barefaced counterfeit I ever saw," I said. "You certainly did not get this in person."

The owner of the bogus signature explained. "I had just bought this copy of *Hustler* and was admiring the nude photos of Jackie when who

2

2. *Jacqueline Kennedy Onassis (autograph note signed)*

should stroll by but Jackie herself. Instantly I thought, What a coup if I could get her to sign a nude photo! At that moment a youngster about fourteen years old walked up and I said, 'That's Jackie Onassis who just passed and if you can get her signature on here'—and I pointed to this photo—'I'll give you fifty dollars.' He grabbed the magazine and was off like a shot after Jackie, who was just turning the corner. Ten minutes later he was back. 'It was pretty tough,' he told me. 'She didn't want to sign at first, but I talked her into it.' I gave him the fifty dollars, of course."

"Well," I said, "if it's any consolation, I think you met a future millionaire today."

A lithesome transition takes us from Jackie O. to the French courtesans, most of whom bequeathed a generous supply of autographs to posterity. But these are quite expensive. Mme. de Pompadour seldom signed her letters. Mme. Du Barry, on the other hand, flooded Paris with her IOUs.

3

4

3. *Mme. de Pompadour*

4. *Mme. Du Barry*

5

5. *Susan B. Anthony*

Recently, with the advent of the women's lib movement, there has been a tremendous rocketing of interest in almost forgotten leaders such as Belva Lockwood, the first woman to run for president, and Susan B. Anthony and Elizabeth Cady Stanton, the great social reformers. Values have increased thirty-fold in the past decade and, in my opinion, are slated to go much higher.

See key to abbreviations, p. 11.

	SIG.	DS/LS	ALS	SP *
Bella Abzug	$5	$10	$15	$10
Abigail Adams	90	175	325	—
Jane Addams	8	20	65	25
Susan B. Anthony	15	50	85	55
Elizabeth Arden	10	20	25	25
Clara Barton	30	55	85	60
Amelia Bloomer	25	75	125	85
Anne Boleyn	1200	3500	6000	—

	SIG.	DS/LS	ALS	SP *
Belle Boyd	$100	$300	$550	$400
Eva Braun	125	275	500	400
Nan Britton	15	40	60	100
Rosalynn Carter	7	10	15	10
Edith Cavell	100	175	275	—
Mme. Chiang Kai-shek	10	20	75	15
Colette	15	50	125	75
Charlotte Corday	—	—	5500	—
Pauline Cushman	125	250	400	300
Dorothea Dix	10	30	50	35
Mme. Du Barry	100	300	475	—
Mamie Eisenhower	8	12	18	12
Elizabeth Ford	10	15	35	15
Barbara Fritchie	—	425	—	—
Hetty Green	15	35	85	50
Nell Gwyn	400	1800	—	—
Lady Emma Hamilton	100	350	450	—
Patty Hearst	35	50	75	—
Martha Jefferson	450	1800	2750	—
Joan of Arc	—	50,000	—	—
Lady Bird Johnson	7	12	20	15
Osa Johnson	7	10	15	12
Helen Keller	15	50	85	55
Mary Lincoln	135	600	850	350
Belva Lockwood	25	85	110	150
Clare Boothe Luce	5	10	15	10
Dolley Madison	50	150	275	—
Mme. de Maintenon	90	250	550	—
Mary, Queen of Scots	1500	3500	8500	—
Mata Hari	125	250	400	300
Margaret Mead	7	15	20	10
Carry Nation	15	35	60	75
Florence Nightingale	30	85	150	100
Patricia Nixon	8	12	25	20
Tricia Nixon	3	10	12	10
Jacqueline Kennedy Onassis	50	100	300	85
Eva Perón	25	75	100	35
Lydia E. Pinkham	75	100	175	—
Mme. de Pompadour	150	325	600	—
Emily Post	10	20	30	20
Elizabeth Ray	5	20	35	25
Eleanor Roosevelt	5	15	45	25
Betsy Ross	—	8000	—	—
George Sand	20	35	75	100

	SIG.	DS/LS	ALS	SP *
Clara Schumann	$25	$70	$100	$ —
Elizabeth Cady Stanton	8	25	45	35
Gloria Steinem	3	10	10	10
Bess Truman	7	10	20	10
Gloria Vanderbilt	3	8	15	15
Cosima Wagner	30	60	150	100
Dr. Mary E. Walker	15	35	75	75
Martha Washington	375	850	3500	—
Frances E. Willard	10	30	50	25
Wallis Windsor	10	35	85	45

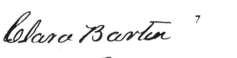

6. *Abigail Adams*

7. *Clara Barton*

8. *Belle Boyd*

9. *Eva Braun*

10. *Nan Britton*

11. *Colette*

12. *Dorothea Dix*

13. *Pauline Cushman (autograph letter signed)*

14. *Mamie Doud Eisenhower*

15. *Barbara Fritchie*

16. *Nell Gwyn*

17. *Lady Emma Hamilton*

18. *Martha Jefferson*

19. *Joan of Arc*

20. *Mme. de Maintenon*

21. *Helen Keller (autograph note signed)*

22. *Lady Bird Johnson*

23. *Mary Lincoln*

24. *Dolley Madison*

25. *Mata Hari*

26. *Eva Perón (note signed)*

16 The mark of Ellinor — E G Gwyn Madam Gwyn

19 Jehanne

17 Emma Hamilton

18 Martha Jefferson

20 MAINTENON

21 Lovingly yours Helen Keller

Please excuse this hastily written note. Helen

22 Lady Bird Johnson

24 D P Madison

23 Mary Lincoln

25 Mata=Hari

26 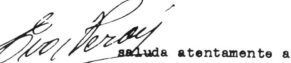 saluda atentamente a Gran Bretaña Don Sir John Balfour y Sra. y presarles su agradecimiento por las flores deseándole pronto restablecimiento.

27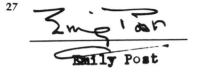

29

28

Florence Nightingale.

30

31

32

33

34

35

36

27. *Emily Post*

28. *Florence Nightingale*

29. *Pat Nixon*

30. *Eleanor Roosevelt*

31. *George Sand*

32. *Wallis Windsor*

33. *Bess W. Truman*

34. *Cosima Wagner*

35. *Clara Schumann*

36. *Dr. Mary E. Walker*

Presidents

A COLLECTION OF LETTERS and documents of the presidents is a history of the United States in miniature. And all of the presidents are readily available, provided you have the necessary funds. That is, unless you choose to collect their autographs signed while in office. The two stumbling blocks to such a collection are William Henry Harrison, who served only one bed-ridden month as president, and James A. Garfield, shot after an administration of less than four months. Their autographs during other periods of their distinguished careers are not difficult to get.

Some of the presidents were gratifyingly prolific, pouring out tens of thousands of letters. The two Roosevelts and Hoover peppered the nation with their missives, many of them very interesting. Coolidge, it might be added, never wrote an interesting letter and Harry Truman and John Adams never a dull one.

On land grants, signatures of Madison, Monroe, John Quincy Adams and Andrew Jackson are so common that every time I hear the crackle of parchment I suspect it is someone bringing a few such old documents into my galleries. The early presidents were required by law to sign all ships' papers, or authorizations for American vessels to sail under our flag, and these picturesque documents are avidly sought by collectors. Some are ornate, on parchment. Others are on paper in three or four languages. Most of the early ships' papers were signed by two presidents, one of them being at the time secretary of state.

There is a great interest today in franking signatures (used to send mail free) of the early presidents. The franking privilege was abolished in 1877. High prices are often paid for letter covers franked by Washington, Adams, Jefferson, Lincoln and other rare or desirable presidents.

For those interested in financial documents, a collection of presidential checks is very appealing. Most of them are available except for Zachary Taylor, Franklin Pierce and all of the presidents after Truman.

1

1. *Address leaf franked by George Washington*

2

Bank of the United States, July 6. *1793.*

PAY to *Henry Pepper — ,, — * or Bearer,

twenty seven dollars and sixty seven cents of **Dollars.**

27. **DOLLARS** *67 cents*

2. *Bank check of Thomas Jefferson*

Since the administration of John F. Kennedy, all presidents have made use of the autopen. Presidents no longer personally sign their mail or any souvenir items, such as photographs, and it is now apparent that President Carter is employing a new device, the Signa-Signer, which can write a short letter in pen and ink.

Usually when I tell a collector that he owns a machine-signed letter or photograph, his reaction is at first one of incredulity, then anger at the deception by the president. Not long ago a young man brought me his most prized possession, a photograph bearing the signature of President Kennedy. "I'm sorry to tell you," I said, "but this was signed by autopen."

THE WHITE HOUSE
WASHINGTON

3

And so, my fellow Americans: ask not what your country can do for you... ask what you can do for your country.

3. *Statement from Kennedy's Inaugural Address, which fetched $11,000 at a Hamilton auction*

"It just happens I saw the president sign it," he replied.

"A machine signed this photo," I repeated. "I know the autopen pattern well and have seen it hundreds of times."

"Well," admitted my visitor, "I didn't exactly see Kennedy sign it. His secretary took the photo into his office and brought it back with this signature on it. Are you positive it's not genuine?"

"I am."

The young man walked to my wastebasket and deliberately, almost defiantly, tore into tiny pieces the photograph signed by Kennedy's robot.

Leonard Lyons, the columnist, once noticed in the window of my gallery a display of signed presidential photos, featuring John F. Kennedy, then president, at $65, more than a U. S. Grant at $55. Lyons wrote to Kennedy and told him about it. "Dear Leonard," replied the president, "I appreciate your letter about the market in Kennedy signatures. It is hard to believe that the going price is so high now. In order not to depress the market any further, I will not sign this letter."

Two of the most famed American philographers were John F. Kennedy and Franklin D. Roosevelt, both of whom specialized in American historical documents.

* See key to abbreviations, p. 11.

	SIG.	DS/LS	ALS	SP *
George Washington	$625	$2000	$2800	$—
John Adams	275	850	1200	—
Thomas Jefferson	250	700	1400	—
James Madison	75	225	650	—
James Monroe	60	210	400	—
John Quincy Adams	50	150	300	—
Andrew Jackson	65	210	500	—
Martin Van Buren	35	125	150	1200
William Henry Harrison	50	250	500	—
John Tyler	40	125	210	1100
James K. Polk	100	325	475	—
Zachary Taylor	90	225	600	—
Millard Fillmore	35	110	135	900
Franklin Pierce	35	100	125	900
James Buchanan	45	140	160	900
Abraham Lincoln	300	800	1400	2700
Andrew Johnson	50	165	375	450
Ulysses S. Grant	35	90	150	275
Rutherford B. Hayes	35	90	175	300
James A. Garfield	40	110	150	250
Chester A. Arthur	65	200	225	350

	SIG.	DS/LS	ALS	SP *
Grover Cleveland	$35	$85	$135	$125
Benjamin Harrison	40	85	140	250
William McKinley	40	100	225	250
Theodore Roosevelt	30	75	200	150
William Howard Taft	25	50	140	80
Woodrow Wilson	50	140	300	125
Warren G. Harding	65	90	250	175
Calvin Coolidge	25	85	400	100
Herbert Hoover	20	35	600	60
Franklin D. Roosevelt	40	50	350	80
Harry S Truman	25	50	550	50
Dwight D. Eisenhower	40	125	750	75
John F. Kennedy	150	300	900	350
Lyndon B. Johnson	75	150	2000	125
Richard M. Nixon	60	150	2000	150
Gerald R. Ford	35	125	1000	80
Jimmy Carter	50	150	650	75

Note: The autographs of the Watergate personalities—obviously not presidents themselves, but so closely identified with the presidency that we mention them here—are all of about the same value. Dean, Ehrlichman, Mitchell, and other conspirators are worth $5 for a signature, around $10 for a typed letter signed, and up to $50 for an interesting handwritten letter.

4

5

6

7

4. *George Washington, age seventeen*

5. *George Washington, as president*

6. *Thomas Jefferson*

7. *John Adams*

8. *James Madison*

9. *James Monroe*

10. *John Quincy Adams*

11. *Martin Van Buren*

12. *Andrew Jackson*

13. *William Henry Harrison*

14. *John Tyler*

15. *James K. Polk*

16. *Zachary Taylor*

17. *Millard Fillmore*

18. *Franklin Pierce*

19

Executive Mansion
Sep. 14. 1861
Hon. Sec. of Treasury
    My dear Sir;
        Mr. Thomas Alsop,
is my personal acquaintance
of near twenty years standing,
and one of the truest men
I ever knew— He is needy, now,
and if you can at once, or
in a reasonable time, find
a clerkship for him, I shall
be greatly obliged to you—
        Yours truly
        A. Lincoln

19. *Abraham Lincoln (autograph letter signed)*

20. *James Buchanan*

21. *Andrew Johnson*

22. *U. S. Grant*

23. *Rutherford B. Hayes*

20

James Buchanan

21

Andrew Johnson

22 *U. S. Grant*   **23** *R B Hayes*

24. *James A. Garfield*

25. *Chester A. Arthur*

26. *Grover Cleveland*

27. *Benjamin Harrison*

28. *William McKinley*

29. *Theodore Roosevelt (autograph quotation signed)*

24

25

26

27

28

29 *Courage, honesty and common sense are essential to good citizenship; joined with courtesy, and consideration for others.*

Theodore Roosevelt

april 8th 1911

30

31

32

33

34

35

36

37

38

30. *William Howard Taft*

31. *Woodrow Wilson*

32. *Warren G. Harding*

33. *Calvin Coolidge*

34. *Herbert Hoover*

35. *Franklin D. Roosevelt*

36. *Harry S Truman*

37. *Dwight D. Eisenhower*

38. *John F. Kennedy*

39. *Lyndon B. Johnson*

40. *Richard M. Nixon*

41. *Gerald R. Ford, as congressman*

42. *Gerald R. Ford, as president*

43. *Jimmy Carter, as presidential candidate*

44. *Jimmy Carter, as president (autograph note signed)*

39

40

41

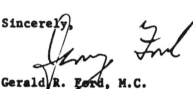

Sincerely,

Gerald R. Ford, M.C.

43

42

44

3-21-77

To Cabinet & other Officers

Submit the paperwork reduction recommendations on time (3/31/77)

Respectfully

Jimmy Carter

45

Sincerely,

John F. Kennedy

Sincerely yours,

JOHN F. KENNEDY

Very sincerely yours,

John F. Kennedy

45. *The Most Unpredictable Signature in History—John F. Kennedy's. Bewildering in its variability, President Kennedy's signature was erratic and unreadable. The only consistent signatures of Kennedy are the seven known robot patterns, the fabrications of the eighteen secretaries who signed letters and photos for him, and the counterfeits of three different forgers.*

46

Yours sincerely,

46. *John D. Ehrlichman*

The Rise and Fall of Three Powerful Men Traced in Their Signatures

1. *Napoleon (1804), a newly elected emperor*

2. *Napoleon (1809), the most powerful man in Europe*

3. *Napoleon (1815), after Waterloo, defeated and broken*

4. *Adolf Hitler (1932), on the verge of becoming führer*

5. *Adolf Hitler (1936), a dictator, wielding enormous power*

6. *Adolf Hitler (December, 1944), injured by a would-be assassin, his armies crushed, soon to commit suicide. Actual size.*

7. *Richard Nixon (1955), an ambitious vice president. Notice the striking similarity between the capital Ns of Nixon and Napoleon.*

8. *Richard Nixon (1973), a re-elected president, at the zenith of his popularity and success*

9. *Richard Nixon (1974), after Watergate, stripped of his power and facing impeachment*

From success to failure, a study in the disintegration of personality and character under pressure. In all three terminal signatures there seems to be a subconscious effort to conceal the identity by making the signature totally unreadable.

1

2

3

4

5

6

7

Sincerely,

Richard Nixon

8

9

Jewish Leaders

YOU DON'T HAVE TO BE JEWISH to enjoy the excitement of collecting Judaica, especially American Judaica. I well recall the exhilaration I felt when I first held in my hands a batch of intimate letters of Rebecca Gratz, the beautiful Philadelphian whom Washington Irving adored, Sully painted, and Sir Walter Scott made into the heroine of *Ivanhoe.* Her letters are highly prized.

1

1. *Rebecca Gratz*

The Jews played a vital role in the Revolutionary War and the letters and documents of Haym Salomon, Aaron Lopez and other merchants who helped to finance the Continental Army are eagerly sought by discerning philographers. Few Revolutionary autographs fetch as much as Salomon's, and I venture to say that if a significant letter from his pen were to turn up it would fetch far more than a comparable letter of Washington or Jefferson.

2

2. *Haym Salomon*

3

3. *Maxwell Bodenheim*

While I have always had a special fondness for the flamboyant Max Bodenheim and have read with delight many of the impromptu ballads which he swapped for booze in Greenwich Village, my favorite character is the picturesque Joshua A. Norton, a former San Francisco rice broker and self-proclaimed Emperor Norton I of the United States. His colorful garb—a blue military uniform with enormous epaulettes and studded with great brass buttons—and his mode of transportation—an impressively large bicycle—gave him the grandeur to suit his numerous proclamations. Most intriguing were his imperial bank notes, all warranted by his personal signature, and often accepted at face value by the amused

4

4. Norton I bank note

merchants of San Francisco. They thought they were doing the "emperor" a favor by cashing his bank notes for fifty cents, but these notes have proved a sound investment and are today worth several hundred times their face value.

* See key to abbreviations, p. 11.

	SIG.	DS/LS	ALS *
Felix Adler	$5	$10	$15
Bernard Baruch	8	15	30
David Ben-Gurion	25	60	150
Judah P. Benjamin	30	175	275
Léon Blum	5	15	25
Maxwell Bodenheim	10	25	40
Louis D. Brandeis	25	75	125
Martin Buber	20	50	75
Benjamin Cardozo	20	65	125
Moshe Dayan	5	15	75
Benjamin Disraeli	40	70	135
Isaac Disraeli	10	35	35
Alfred Dreyfus	50	130	200
Abba Eban	5	15	50
Felix Frankfurter	20	65	100
Col. Isaac Franks	75	200	400
Samuel Gompers	10	30	50
Bernard Gratz	65	150	300
Michael Gratz	60	150	275
Rebecca Gratz	60	120	200

	SIG.	DS/LS	ALS *
Theodor Herzl	$150	$275	$ 500
Vladimir Jabotinsky	60	200	300
Emma Lazarus	75	160	350
Herbert H. Lehman	3	5	7
Uriah P. Levy	75	225	350
Aaron Lopez	50	150	425
Moses Mendelssohn	50	185	350
Henry Morgenthau, Jr.	7	12	25
Mordecai M. Noah	30	80	200
Major Benjamin Nones	75	150	225
Norton I (J. A. Norton)	100	250	350
Adolph Ochs	10	40	65
Jonas Phillips	50	150	250
Yitzhak Rabin	5	15	65
Julius Rosenwald	10	20	35
Meyer A. Rothschild	85	175	375
Haym Salomon	400	1500	3500
David Sarnoff	5	20	25
Moses Seixas	50	150	325
Mordecai Sheftall	50	150	260
Baruch Spinoza	350	1200	4500
Arthur Hays Sulzberger	7	15	25
Henrietta Szold	25	55	110
Chaim Weizmann	85	200	425
Rabbi Stephen S. Wise	3	10	15
David L. Yulee	12	35	50

6   5

acting Secretary of War.

7

8

9

5. *Judah P. Benjamin*

6. *Louis D. Brandeis*

7. *Martin Buber*

8. *David Ben-Gurion*

9. *Benjamin N. Cardozo*

10. *Moshe Dayan*

11. *Bernard Gratz*

12. *Isaac D'Israeli (or Disraeli)*

13. *Benjamin Disraeli*

14. *Alfred Dreyfus*

15. *Theodor Herzl (autograph note signed)*

16. *Uriah P. Levy*

17. *Felix Frankfurter*

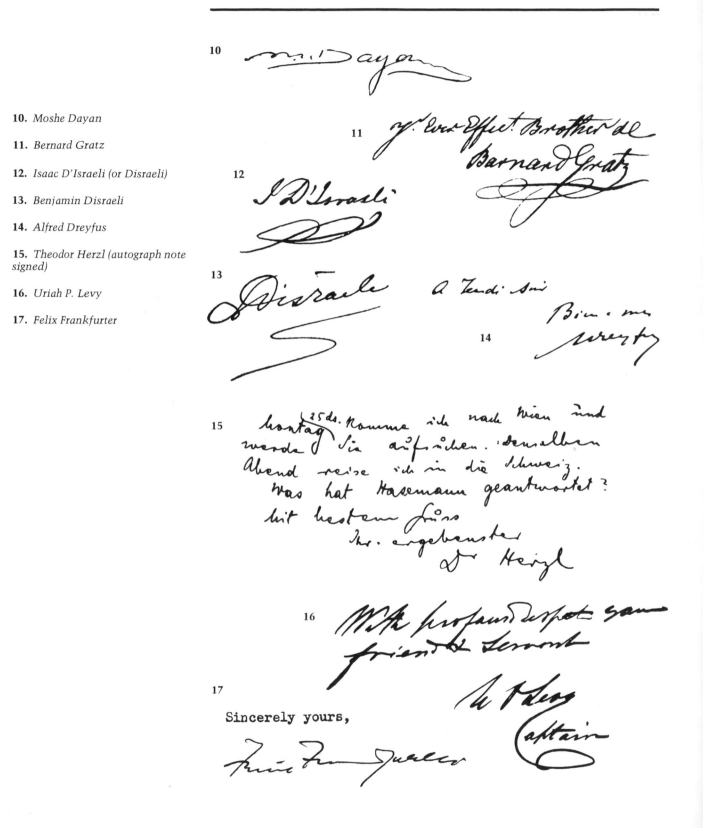

18

18. *Emma Lazarus*

19. *Aaron Lopez*

20. *Moses Mendelssohn*

21. *Mordecai M. Noah*

22. *Henrietta Szold*

23. *Moses Seixas*

24. *Mordecai Sheftall*

25. *Baruch Spinoza*

26. *Chaim Weizmann*

19

20

21

22

23

24

25

26

Signers
of the
Declaration
of Independence

A DOCUMENT SIGNED by the obscure Button Gwinnett is worth 100 times as much as a document of the great Thomas Jefferson. The difference is one of rarity, not of greatness. Gwinnett's life was snuffed out in a duel shortly after he signed the Declaration, whereas Jefferson lived on for half a century to the very day.

Among the signers of the Declaration, rarity is what makes value and the endless search goes on for the scarce names. Fierce battles are waged in the auction room for rare signers. A letter of Gwinnett once fell to the highest bidder at $51,000.

The Southerners have cornered the market on rarity. Gwinnett of Georgia, Lynch and Middleton of South Carolina, and Hewes, Penn and Hooper of North Carolina are hard to come by. George Taylor of Pennsylvania stands forth in solitary prominence as the only Northern signer whose autograph is truly rare.

If a letter or document bears the magic date of 1776, the value doubles, often quadruples. The closer you get to July 4, the more valuable the document.

About a year ago an elderly man walked into my gallery, introduced himself, and announced that he and his wife were experts in handwriting and had discovered that Franklin forged all the signatures on the Declaration of Independence. I said, "Are you aware that some of the most skilled forgers who ever lived spent their creative lives trying to forge successfully just one or two signers—and I can spot their fabrications clear across a room? How do you suppose it possible for one man, without at least three centuries of practice, to forge so perfectly fifty-five signatures?"

My visitor changed his approach. "He did it because it was not safe for all fifty-six members of the Congress to be in the same room at the same time."

I looked at this adventurer from the lunatic fringe with new interest. "How the devil do you imagine they got together to confer on official business and pass laws?" I asked.

He did not answer this, but went on. "Franklin could forge these signatures," he explained, "because in those days there was no law against forgery."

"You'd better look up your history," I said. "In some of the colonies the penalty was cutting off the right hand of the forger. In others it was hanging."

"My wife and I have spent five years studying the Declaration of Independence," persisted the Ancient Mariner, "and we are positive that Franklin signed all the names on it. May I have an opinion from you to use in our publicity?"

"Sir," I said sternly, "you are everlastingly bombed out of your mind. You need to have your cranial contents scrutinized by a competent alienist."

"May I quote you?" he asked.

"Of course, of course," I said, as I showed him to the door.

1

1. *Original manuscript epitaph of Benjamin Franklin, written at age twenty-two*

*See key to abbreviations, p. 11.

	SIG.	DS/LS	ALS *
John Adams	$275	$850	$1200
Samuel Adams	125	400	1200
Josiah Bartlett	75	350	550
Carter Braxton	90	400	650
Charles Carroll	55	150	300
Samuel Chase	75	150	400
Abraham Clark	125	450	750
George Clymer	50	150	225
William Ellery	65	150	275

	SIG.	DS/LS	ALS *
William Floyd	$75	$175	$350
Benjamin Franklin	350	1300	3500
Elbridge Gerry	80	200	500
Button Gwinnett	4000	60,000	125,000
Lyman Hall	350	900	1500
John Hancock	250	650	1000
Benjamin Harrison	80	150	300
John Hart	75	225	3500
Joseph Hewes	550	1500	3500
Thomas Heyward, Jr.	55	150	450
William Hooper	700	2500	4500
Stephen Hopkins	90	250	350
Francis Hopkinson	75	250	400
Samuel Huntington	50	100	300
Thomas Jefferson	250	700	1400
Francis Lightfoot Lee	500	950	3000
Richard Henry Lee	100	300	750
Francis Lewis	90	250	650
Philip Livingston	85	175	500
Thomas Lynch, Jr.	4000	10,000	100,000
Thomas McKean	50	150	400
Arthur Middleton	500	1700	2500
Lewis Morris	90	225	400
Robert Morris	50	125	200
John Morton	70	150	3000
Thomas Nelson, Jr.	75	300	650
William Paca	125	325	750
Robert Treat Paine	90	250	600
John Penn	250	650	1500
George Read	50	100	225
Caesar Rodney	60	175	250
George Ross	50	125	250
Benjamin Rush	125	350	700
Edward Rutledge	60	130	300
Roger Sherman	50	125	250
James Smith	60	150	325
Richard Stockton	100	500	1200
Thomas Stone	75	175	425
George Taylor	1000	2750	5000
Matthew Thornton	80	200	450
George Walton	50	125	250
William Whipple	85	225	500
William Williams	50	125	250
James Wilson	65	150	300

	SIG.	DS/LS	ALS *
John Witherspoon	$ 300	$ 700	$1000
Oliver Wolcott	75	150	400
George Wythe	175	700	1250

2

Philadelphia October 7th 1776

Gentlemen

The Committee Appointed to carry into Execution, the Inclosed Resolve, can think of no method so proper for the State of Newyork, as to apply to the Convention, and for that purpose we do send you ten thousand dollars, and desire you to appoint proper person in the several Districts to Execute the same; and if upon trial you find that more Cloathing may be had than this money will purchase you may 'ave more by applying to this Committee.—

To the

To the hon.ble the Convention of the State of Newyork

2. *Letter dated 1776 bearing the signatures of nine signers of the Declaration of Independence: Robert Treat Paine, Josiah Bartlett, William Ellery, William Williams, George Wythe, Arthur Middleton, William Floyd, Lyman Hall and George Ross. This remarkable letter is worth at least $25,000.*

3. *Signatures of the signers of the Declaration of Independence as they appear on the original Declaration*

3

Francis Lightfoot Lee

Carter Braxton Benj. Harrison

Casar Rodney Th. Nelson jr

Geo. Read Matthew Thornton

Tho. M. Kean Step Hopkins

Edward Rutledge William Ellery

Roger Sherman

Tho. Heyward Junr

Thomas Lynch Junr

Arthur Middleton Charles Carroll of Carrollton

Geo Clymer

George Wythe Jas Smith

Sam a Huntington

Richard Henry Lee Wm Williams

Josiah Bartlett Oliver Wolcott

Wm Whipple John Adams

Saml Adams Robt Treat Paine

Th Jefferson Elbridge Gerry

Black Leaders

ONE SUMMER AFTERNOON about ten years ago a tall, handsome man with a beautiful girl at his side breezed into my gallery and asked, laughing, "Anybody want my autograph?" There were five or six persons in the gallery and we all recognized the dashing Adam Clayton Powell, but everyone was too embarrassed to ask for his signature. Just last week one of the collectors who was present said ruefully, "I wish I'd got his autograph. It's too late now."

1

1. *Adam Clayton Powell*

Today the collecting of letters and documents of black leaders, political and cultural, is extremely popular and even slave deeds of sale, once ignored by philographers, are keenly sought after. Frederick Douglass letters which only a few years ago sold for a dollar or two now fetch $75 or $100. But a word of caution: Douglass, like Booker T. Washington and Martin Luther King, Jr., employed many secretaries to sign his letters.

An enthusiastic collector of black documents is the distinguished actor Harry Belafonte.

2

2. *Martin Luther King, Jr.*

3

In a composite nation like ours, made up of almost every variety of the human family, there should be, as before the law no rich, no poor, no high, no low, no black, no white, but one country, one citizenship, equal rights and a common destiny for all.

A government that cannot or does not protect the humblest citizen in his right to life, liberty and the pursuit of happiness, should be reformed or overthrown, without delay.

Fred'k Douglass

Washington D.C. Oct 20. 1883.

3. *Frederick Douglass (autograph quotation signed)*

* *See key to abbreviations, p. 11.*

	SIG.	DS/LS	ALS *
Ralph Abernathy	$7	$12	$25
James Baldwin	10	30	45
Thomas Bradley	3	10	15
Edward W. Brooke	5	10	15
Gwendolyn Brooks	5	15	25
Ralph J. Bunche	7	15	20
George Washington Carver	25	55	100
Shirley Chisholm	3	10	15
Henri Christophe	125	400	850
Countee Cullen	30	55	90
Gen. Benjamin O. Davis, Jr.	3	8	15

	SIG.	DS/LS	ALS *
Jean Jacques Dessalines	$ 125	$ 375	$ 850
Father Divine	10	20	35
Frederick Douglass	50	110	225
Paul Laurence Dunbar	35	80	110
James Farmer	5	15	30
Haile Selassie	75	225	475
Alex Haley	10	25	50
Mathew A. Henson	20	45	75
Langston Hughes	20	60	100
Gen. Daniel James, Jr.	3	8	15
James Weldon Johnson	25	65	100
Martin Luther King, Jr.	150	250	1000
Malcolm X	85	150	400
Thurgood Marshall	8	15	30
Elijah Muhammad	35	100	250
Adam Clayton Powell	10	25	40
Hiram R. Revels	20	35	50
J. J. Roberts	35	150	250
Paul Robeson	10	20	45
Carl Stokes	3	10	15
Touissant l'Ouverture	125	375	850
Sojourner Truth	150	325	750
Harriet Tubman	85	175	325
Booker T. Washington	15	35	110
Phillis Wheatley	200	450	900
Roy Wilkins	5	10	15
Richard Wright	12	40	60
Frank Yerby	8	20	40

4

5

6

7

4. *Ralph J. Bunche*

5. *Gwendolyn Brooks*

6. *Henri Christophe*

7. *George Washington Carver*

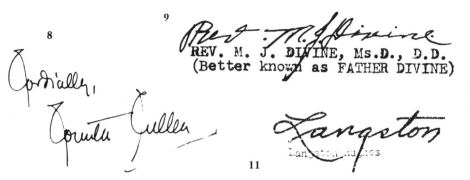

REV. M. J. DIVINE, Ms.D., D.D.
(Better known as FATHER DIVINE)

8. *Countee Cullen*

9. *Father Divine*

10. *James Weldon Johnson (autograph note signed)*

11. *Langston Hughes*

12. *Phillis Wheatley*

13. *J. J. Roberts*

14. *Touissant l'Ouverture*

15. *Haile Selassie*

16. *Booker T. Washington*

Jurists,
Lawyers,
and Financiers

HENRY FORD, the world's richest man, literally found himself without a cent as he sought to buy a penny stamp for a postcard. The mail clerk obligingly accepted Ford's check for one cent and within a few days had sold it to a collector for $500. It was still a bargain, for today that famous check is worth at least $1000.

1

1. *Henry Ford*

One of the most avid philographers of modern times, J. P. Morgan, began collecting the signatures of Methodist-Episcopal bishops when he was a boy. His collection of bishops is still incomplete, but the priceless manuscripts and letters of famous authors which he assembled are among the world's supreme cultural treasures, surpassing even those of Henry E. Huntington of California.

The chief justices form an interesting group and are not hard to assemble. The most valuable are the letters of John Marshall and John Jay, and the rarest in full handwritten letters is E. D. White.

2

2. *John Jay*

Curiously, the most vehemently discussed document in history is not the Declaration of Independence but the disputed holographic will of billionaire Howard Hughes.

3

New York Decr 8th 1864

My dear Stevens

Yours if 6th ult.

I am willing to pay the $50 to Bassett. Provided he will agree to send us _very_ _sorely_ _two_ _copies_ of every document published for Com — mittees of ways + means. + finance committee — both when first reported + when printed as passed. —

You can pay him if you think it safe to do so in advance — but the whole thing is useless unless. we can depend upon it being faithfully carried out yours truly

J Pierpont Morgan

3. *J. Pierpont Morgan (autograph letter signed)*

* *See key to abbreviations, p. 11.*

	SIG.	DS/LS	ALS	SP *
John Jacob Astor	$ 35	$ 90	$150	$ —
F. Lee Bailey	5	10	15	8
Melvin Belli	5	10	15	8
Nicholas Biddle	15	30	40	—
Sir William Blackstone	150	475	900	—
"Diamond Jim" Brady	50	100	200	—
Warren E. Burger	5	12	25	10
Andrew Carnegie	15	25	35	40
Salmon P. Chase	10	35	65	75
Walter P. Chrysler	20	75	150	50
Sir Edward Coke	125	325	700	—
Jay Cooke	7	20	30	15
Peter Cooper	10	35	75	50
Clarence Darrow	35	75	150	75
William O. Douglas	5	12	20	8
Oliver Ellsworth	30	65	125	—
Harvey S. Firestone	20	55	80	35
James Fisk	15	35	50	25
Henry Ford	100	250	900	275
H. C. Frick	20	50	85	60
Melville W. Fuller	8	25	70	35
Albert Gallatin	25	45	110	—
J. Paul Getty	12	40	65	30
Stephen Girard	50	110	185	—
Arthur J. Goldberg	3	10	20	8
Jay Gould	20	55	65	75
Hugo Grotius	175	425	800	—
Alexander Hamilton	75	200	500	—
Andrew Hamilton	60	175	450	—
E. H. Harriman	20	35	50	25
William Randolph Hearst	10	25	45	25
James J. Hill	20	55	75	50
Oliver Wendell Holmes, Jr.	25	65	100	75
Charles Evans Hughes	8	15	35	15
Howard Hughes	50	110	350	150
Henry E. Huntington	25	35	60	—
Robert G. Ingersoll	5	12	15	15
John Jay	85	175	310	—
Alfred Krupp	65	125	175	—
John Law	100	325	600	—
John Marshall	75	250	475	—

	SIG.	DS/LS	ALS	SP *
Andrew W. Mellon	$ 7	$15	$ 65	$ 25
J. P. Morgan, Sr.	50	110	225	175
Stavros Niarchos	15	40	65	25
Louis Nizer	5	10	15	8
Aristotle Onassis	25	65	125	80
George Peabody	15	40	75	—
John D. Rockefeller, Sr.	25	60	225	85
John Rutledge	50	150	185	—
Russell Sage	15	35	50	30
Leland Stanford	20	45	55	—
Harlan F. Stone	10	35	75	35
Joseph Story	10	30	60	—
Roger B. Taney	20	75	135	—
Cornelius Vanderbilt	25	60	100	—
Frederick M. Vinson	10	40	75	25
John Wanamaker	5	10	30	25
Earl Warren	10	35	75	20
George Westinghouse	20	75	175	75
Edward D. White	20	35	250	75
Frank W. Woolworth	30	65	150	—

4

5

6

7

8

4. *John Jacob Astor*

5. *Sir William Blackstone*

6. *Peter Cooper*

7. *Andrew Carnegie*

8. *Clarence Darrow*

9

[signature: Respectfully Jay Gould]

10

[signature: O. Ellsworth]

11

[signature: J. Paul Getty]

12

[handwritten quotation: To see so far as one may, and to feel, the great forces that are behind every detail — for that makes all the difference between philosophy and gossip, between great action and small; the least wavelet of the Atlantic ocean is mightier than one of Buzzard's Bay — to hammer out as compact and solid a piece of work as one can, to try to make it first rate, and to leave it unadvertised. — O. W. Holmes]

13

[signature: Stephen Girard]

14

[signature: Alexander Hamilton, Secretary of the Treasury]

15

[signature: Charles E. Hughes]

16

Richmond May 4th 34

Dear Sir

In compliance with the request of Mr. Meade I take the liberty to put a letter for him under cover to you and am dear Sir with great esteem Your obedt.

J Marshall

17

18 H. Hamilton

19

20 John D. Rockefeller.

21 J. Rutledge

22

23 Joseph Story

24 R. B. Taney

25

26

16. *John Marshall (autograph letter signed)*

17. *John Law*

18. *Andrew Hamilton*

19. *Stavros Niarchos*

20. *John D. Rockefeller, Sr.*

21. *John Rutledge*

22. *Salmon P. Chase*

23. *Joseph Story*

24. *Roger B. Taney*

25. *Cornelius Vanderbilt*

26. *Earl Warren*

Sports Figures

"Dear Mr. President," wrote a young signature hunter to Herbert Hoover, "would you please send me two autographs? I need two because I want to trade for a Babe Ruth signature and it takes two of yours to get one of his." Hoover sent the two signatures and chuckled for years over the request. He would not, I am sure, be insulted to learn that today a Babe Ruth really is worth two or three Hoovers.

1. *Babe Ruth*

1

Long after all the other players had gone to the showers, Babe Ruth would still be on the field, signing baseballs for youngsters. Most sports heroes were, and are, generous with their signatures—some so hastily scrawled that they are almost impossible to read. Not so with the great pugilist "Gentleman Jim" Corbett. A former bank clerk, Corbett always wrote in a fastidious script that is a model of elegance.

At the turn of the century, when the name of Charles W. Eliot, president of Harvard, was a synonym for erudition, and the name of John L. Sullivan was a synonym for brute strength, a Boston manuscript dealer offered in his catalogue a letter of Eliot at fifty cents and one of Sullivan at a dollar and a half. Reporters rushed to John L. to get his comments on the relative values. "Well," said the Boston Strong Boy, "Goodspeed's an expert. If he says my autograph is worth three times as much as Eliot's, he must be right." Today, not astonishingly, Sullivan's letters sell for at least twenty-five times as much as those of Eliot.

The noted sports announcer Chris Schenkel is a collector of autographs of the great sports personalities of the past.

* See key to abbreviations, p. 11.

	SIG.	DS/LS	ALS	SP *
Hank Aaron	$7	$15	$20	$15
Muhammad Ali	10	20	75	15
Mario Andretti	3	5	10	5
Eddie Arcaro	3	5	7	5
Sammy Baugh	5	7	10	7
Yogi Berra	3	5	10	7

138

2

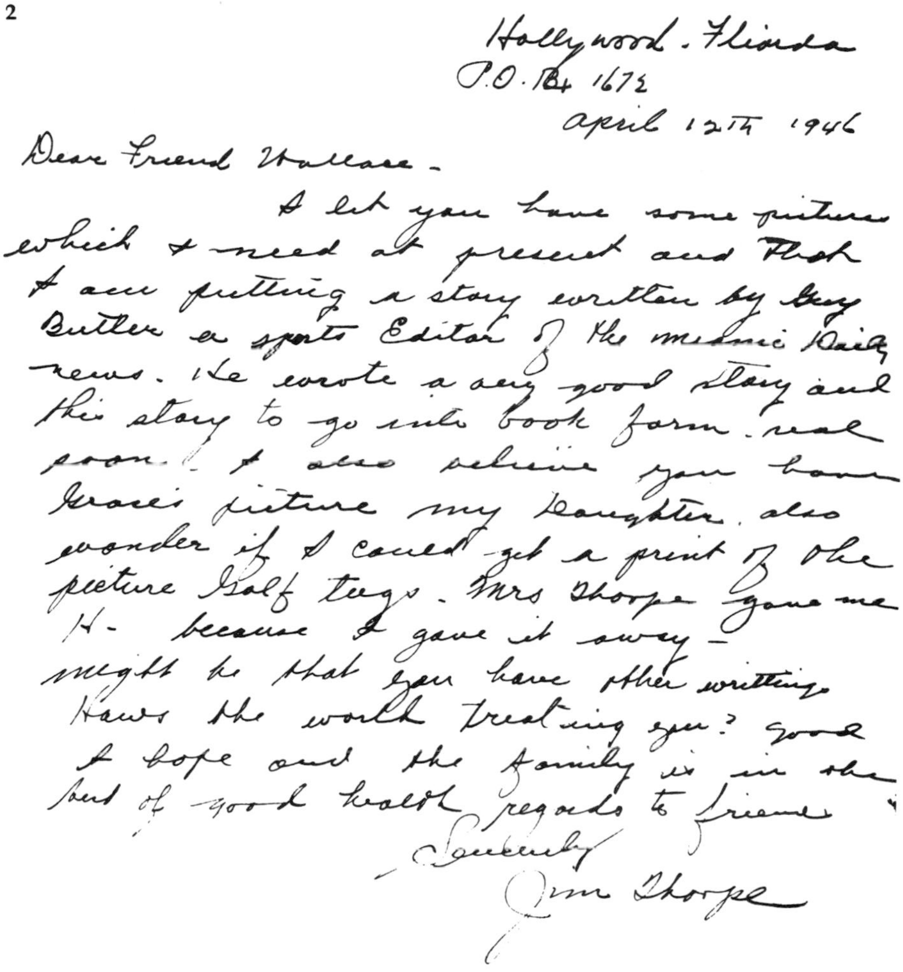

Hollywood. Florida
P.O. Box 1672
April 12th 1946

Dear Friend Wallace -
I let you have some pictures which I need at present and that I am putting a story written by Guy Butler a sports Editor of the Miami Daily news. He wrote a very good story and this story to go into book form - real soon. I also believe you have Grace's picture my daughter. also wonder if I could get a print of the picture Golf togs. Mrs Thorpe gave me it - because I gave it away - might be that you have other writings. Hows the world treating you? good I hope and the family is in the best of good health regards to friends.

Sincerely
Jim Thorpe

2. *Jim Thorpe (autograph letter signed)*

	SIG.	DS/LS	ALS	SP *
George Blanda	$3	$8	$12	$5
Jim Brown	7	15	25	10
Don Budge	5	10	15	7
Walter Camp	10	15	25	15
Wilt Chamberlain	7	12	20	10
Roberto Clemente	15	20	30	15
Ty Cobb	10	20	35	15
James J. Corbett	20	35	75	45
Dizzy Dean	8	12	15	12
Jack Dempsey	5	10	25	10
Babe Didrickson	7	12	15	12
Joe DiMaggio	8	15	35	10
Abner Doubleday	25	50	125	75

	SIG.	DS/LS	ALS	SP *
Leo Durocher	$7	$12	$25	$8
Gertrude Ederle	3	5	8	5
Bob Feller	8	15	20	10
Bob Fitzsimmons	20	30	75	40
A. J. Foyt, Jr.	3	5	10	5
Joe Frazier	7	20	30	15
Lou Gehrig	60	100	225	100
Red Grange	8	20	35	15
Walter Hagen	7	15	20	10
Ben Hogan	3	5	7	5
Reggie Jackson	5	10	20	10
Jack Johnson	25	35	90	45
Bobby Jones	8	15	20	10
Billie Jean King	3	5	7	5
Evel Knievel	3	5	7	5
Strangler Lewis	5	7	10	7
Vince Lombardi	20	25	45	30
Joe Louis	10	25	60	15
Connie Mack	10	20	30	12
Mickey Mantle	5	10	20	10
Rocky Marciano	20	40	75	25
Christy Mathewson	50	85	150	85
Bob Mathias	5	8	15	10
Willy Mays	8	15	20	10
Helen Wills Moody	8	15	20	15
Stan Musial	3	10	12	8
Bronco Nagurski	8	15	25	15
James Naismith	25	50	100	100
Joe Namath	10	15	25	12
Byron Nelson	3	5	8	5
Jack Nicklaus	7	15	30	10
Barney Oldfield	10	25	35	15
Bobby Orr	3	5	7	5
Jesse Owens	5	10	20	10
Satchel Paige	8	15	25	12
Arnold Palmer	5	10	15	8
Richard Petty	3	5	7	5
Grantland Rice	5	10	20	10
Jackie Robinson	15	40	75	25
Sugar Ray Robinson	5	10	20	15
Knute Rockne	30	65	90	75
Bill Russell	5	10	20	10
Babe Ruth	65	150	325	200
Jim Ryun	3	5	7	5

	SIG.	DS/LS	ALS	SP *
Gale Sayers	$5	$8	$10	$8
Tom Seaver	5	10	30	10
Willie Shoemaker	5	10	20	10
Albert Spalding	5	12	25	15
Leon Spinks	5	10	30	10
Amos Alonzo Stagg	10	25	35	15
Bart Starr	3	5	8	5
Casey Stengel	7	15	30	20
John L. Sullivan	30	60	110	75
Jim Thorpe	40	85	130	85
Bill Tilden	8	15	20	15
Lee Trevino	3	7	12	10
Gene Tunney	5	15	30	12
Johnny Unitas	5	10	15	10
Al Unser	3	5	7	5
Pop Warner	10	30	50	25
Johnny Weissmuller	5	10	15	10
Jerry West	3	6	8	5

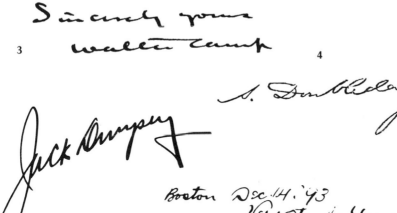

3. *Walter Camp*

4. *Abner Doubleday*

5. *William Harrison "Jack" Dempsey*

6. *Jack Dempsey, "the Nonpareil," from whom the great heavyweight champion William Harrison Dempsey took his nickname, "Jack"*

7. *Joe DiMaggio*

8. *Joe Frazier*

17

18

17. *James J. Corbett*

18. *Bob Feller*

19

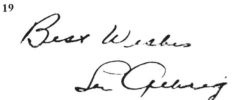

20

19. *Lou Gehrig*

20. *Ben Hogan*

21. *Bobby Jones*

22. *Evel Knievel*

23. *Mickey Mantle*

24. *Willy Mays*

25. *Helen Wills Moody*

26. *Stan Musial*

27. *Byron Nelson*

28. *Jack Nicklaus*

21

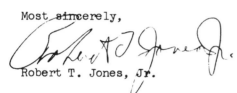

Most sincerely,

Robert T. Jones, Jr.

22

23

24

25

26

27

28

29. *Bobby Orr*

30. *Arnold Palmer*

31. *Grantland Rice*

32. *Sugar Ray Robinson*

33. *Jim Ryun*

34. *Gale Sayers*

35. *Willie Shoemaker*

36. *Bart Starr*

37. *Al Unser*

38. *Johnny Unitas*

39. *Jerry West*

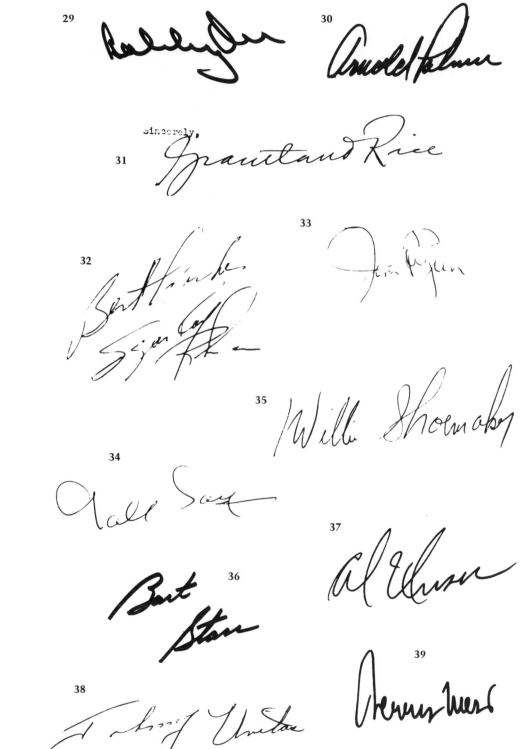

Military and Naval Leaders

THE CLOSER IT HAS BEEN to the smell of gunpowder the more valuable is the letter or document of a great military or naval hero. A battle or campaign letter hastily scrawled on a drumhead may be worth ten or twenty times as much as a pleasant social note penned at leisure on a mahogany desk in the writer's study.

It's almost an axiom that the autographs of men who died in action are rare and costly. This is especially true of younger leaders such as the dashing Confederates Jeb Stuart and Stonewall Jackson, both unknown

1. *J. E. B. Stuart*

2. *T. J. "Stonewall" Jackson*

when the Civil War broke out and both of whom lived only a few short years after attaining fame.

Colorful and dramatic leaders always appeal to philographers. Favorites of World War II collectors are the peppery and fearless George Patton and the spectacular desert fox, Erwin Rommel. Rommel signed his war letters with pencil because ink evaporated so quickly in the fierce African sun.

Very truly yours,

G. S. PATTON, Jr.,
Major General,
Commanding.

Generalleutnant und
Befehlshaber des Deutschen Afrikakorps

3. *George S. Patton, Jr.*

4. *Erwin Rommel*

During World War II, when most military leaders were too busy to send autographs, a collector wrote to General Hap Arnold for his signature and received in reply a printed facsimile. Incensed, the collector sent General Arnold a color photo of a steak dinner, wishing him a pleasant repast. The good-natured Arnold replied with a two-line personal note: "Not synthetic" and a bold signature.

* See key to abbreviations, p. 11.

	SIG.	DS/LS	ALS	SP *
Creighton W. Abrams, Jr.	$3	$10	$15	$10
Emilio Aguinaldo	10	35	40	35
H. H. "Hap" Arnold	5	10	15	15
P. G. T. Beauregard	15	50	125	75
Capt. William Bligh	225	500	1000	—
G. von Blücher	25	75	200	—
Simon Bolivar	100	750	2000	—
Omar N. Bradley	5	10	25	15
Braxton Bragg	25	50	100	60
Capt. George "Beau" Brummell	75	200	375	—
Ambrose E. Burnside	5	25	50	35
Benjamin F. Butler	5	20	45	25
Chiang Kai-shek	10	30	150	25
Robert Clive	90	300	650	—
Stephen Decatur	50	250	500	—
George Dewey	8	15	25	25
Jubal A. Early	10	65	100	50
David G. Farragut	15	50	110	75
Ferdinand Foch	5	25	40	25
N. B. Forrest	150	600	1000	400
John C. Frémont	10	40	85	50
Giuseppe Garibaldi	20	50	75	50
Charles G. "Chinese" Gordon	30	75	100	200
William F. Halsey	10	25	60	15
A. P. Hill	100	350	850	400
Paul von Hindenburg	20	65	100	40
John B. Hood	35	125	200	125
Joseph Hooker	10	25	50	50
O. O. Howard	10	25	60	50
William Hull	60	150	250	—
T. J. "Stonewall" Jackson	250	400	850	750
Joseph Joffre	15	35	75	35
Albert S. Johnston	75	225	600	400

	SIG.	DS/LS	ALS	SP *
Joseph E. Johnston	$15	$40	$85	$50
Philip Kearny	75	200	375	—
E. J. King	8	15	30	15
Robert E. Lee	100	350	650	250
James Longstreet	15	35	100	50
Erich Ludendorff	15	50	100	40
Douglas MacArthur	25	65	200	75
Duke of Marlborough	75	225	350	—
L. J. de Montcalm	150	375	900	—
B. L. Montgomery	15	65	150	50
John S. Mosby	25	50	100	85
Joachim Murat	50	100	225	—
Audie Murphy	25	75	150	75
Lord Nelson	100	300	450	—
Michel Ney	50	125	300	—
George S. Patton	75	150	350	200
Matthew C. Perry	40	85	175	—
Oliver H. Perry	85	300	600	—
John J. Pershing	10	15	35	25
Henri Pétain	15	30	50	40
George E. Pickett	50	125	275	225
Józef Poniatowski	85	350	1200	—
William C. Quantrill	450	1000	2500	—
Erwin Rommel	100	275	350	250
José de San Martín	150	300	800	—
Antonio Lopez de Santa Anna	50	150	275	250
Winfield Scott	10	35	80	50
Philip H. Sheridan	10	35	60	50
William Tecumseh Sherman	10	30	60	50
J. E. B. Stuart	150	300	1500	500
Maxwell D. Taylor	8	20	35	15
George H. Thomas	20	35	75	50
Hideki Tojo	100	200	450	250
Pancho Villa	150	350	1000	400
William Walker	75	125	350	—
Duke of Wellington	15	50	65	—
William C. Westmoreland	5	10	35	15
James Wolfe	165	350	950	—
Isoroku Yamamoto	75	150	300	250
Alvin C. York	15	25	85	35
Georgi K. Zhukov	50	125	300	200

5. *Simón Bolívar*

6. *George "Beau" Brummell*

7. *George Dewey*

8. *Stephen Decatur*

9. *Capt. William Bligh*

10. *N. B. Forrest*

11. *John C. Frémont*

12. *Robert Clive*

13. *David G. Farragut*

14. *Paul von Hindenburg*

15. *William F. Halsey*

16. *E. J. King*

17. *Erich Ludendorff*

18. *Joseph Hooker*

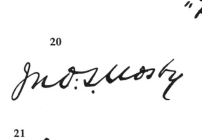

19. *Douglas MacArthur (autograph quotation signed)*

20. *John S. Mosby*

21. *L. J. de Montcalm*

22. *B. L. Montgomery*

23. *Oliver H. Perry*

24. *Robert E. Lee (autograph letter signed, to U. S. Grant, asking for surrender terms)*

25. *James Longstreet*

26. *George E. Pickett*

27. *Matthew C. Perry*

28. *William T. Sherman*

29. *Philip H. Sheridan*

30. *Winfield Scott*

31. *Józef Poniatowski*

32. *John J. Pershing*

33. *A. L. de Santa Anna*

34. *Hideki Tojo*

25

26

27

28

29

30

31

32

33

34

35

I have only stay that I have been more than one hundred times engaged in Battle

Horatio Nelson

36

May the God of Battles crown my Endeavours with success

Nelson & Bronte

37

Yours very truly,

Sgt Alvin C York

Sgt. Alvin C. York.

38

Wellington

39

J Wolfe

40

Wm Walker

41

Sincerely,

Maxwell D Taylor

Maxwell D. Taylor

42

El General en Jefe.

Francisco Villa

35. *Horatio Nelson (autograph note signed with right hand)*

36. *Horatio Nelson (autograph note, signed with left hand after the loss of his right arm in battle)*

37. *Sgt. Alvin C. York*

38. *Duke of Wellington*

39. *James Wolfe*

40. *William Walker*

41. *Maxwell D. Taylor*

42. *Pancho Villa*

Real Men Who Became Fictional

1. *Sir John Falstaff: Sir John Fastolf (1378?–1459), a courageous English soldier who distinguished himself at Agincourt (1415), was transformed by the genius of Shakespeare into an obese and witty poltroon whose antics dominate the stage whenever he appears.*

2. *The Emperor Jones: Henri Christophe (1767–1820), black Haitian king, rose to power by brutality. When his own troops turned on him, he shot himself with a silver bullet. His lurid career was the basis for O'Neill's* The Emperor Jones.

3. *The King of Siam: Mongkut (1804–1868), a progressive king of Siam who modernized his country, was changed into a loveable egomaniac in the celebrated musical,* The King and I.

4. *Cyrano de Bergerac: Cyrano de Bergerac (1619–1655), a French poet and soldier whose unreadable verse and reputed duels inspired Edmond Rostand to invent a romantic and beautiful tragedy around his rather uneventful life.*

5. *Bluebeard: Gilles de Retz (1404–1440), a French marshal who fought under Joan of Arc, murdered and carved up more than 200 little boys in his forest castle before being arrested and executed. From this sadistic monster, Charles Perrault created his great fairy tale "Bluebeard."*

6. *El Cid: Rodrigo Diaz de Bivar (1040?–1099), Spanish soldier of fortune who won great success under Arab kings until overthrown and slain. His real deeds, magnified and romanticized, form the foundation for many imaginary tales of adventure and prowess, including the great Spanish epic,* Poem of the Cid.

7. *C. Auguste Dupin: François Eugène Vidocq (1775–1857), a notorious French criminal who twice escaped from the galleys before reforming and becoming the world's first professional detective, published his incredible* Memoirs *(1828), which may have inspired Hugo's creation of Jean Valjean and certainly did inspire Poe to invent the first fictional detective, C. Auguste Dupin, in "Murders in the Rue Morgue" (1841).*

8. *D'Artagnan: Charles d'Artaignan (1611–1673), a French soldier whose ponderous and rather dull three-volume* Memoirs, *accidently discovered by Alexandre Dumas in an old bookshop, led to the creation of the romantic, swashbuckling hero of* The Three Musketeers.

Values: *Except for Vidocq ($75), Mongkut ($150) and Christophe ($400), the autographs of these colorful men are extremely rare and valuable.*

Criminals
and Outlaws

FROM THE PARANOID JESSE JAMES, who suffered from conjunctivitis and should have been called "Blinkey" James, to the modest Sunday school teacher Lizzie Borden, who may have chopped her parents up with an axe, this is a sorry lot of mortals. But they intrigue historians. Almost without exception, their autographs are rare and sought after. A letter of

1. *Jesse James (autograph note signed)*

2. *Jesse James as Thomas Howard*

3. *Lizzie Borden*

4. *Lee Harvey Oswald, in English and Russian*

5. *John Wilkes Booth*

Oswald is worth twice as much as a comparable letter of John F. Kennedy. John Wilkes Booth outpulls Lincoln, dollar wise, on the autograph market. The anarchist killer Leon Czolgosz, who gunned down McKinley, is holographically worth fifty times as much as his victim.

On a lighter note, few people know that quite a few criminals wrote poetry. The letters of Charles Manson, crudely penciled with many mis-

6. Charles Manson

6

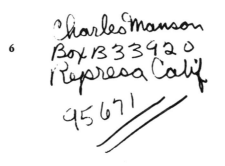

spellings, are darkly poetic and rich in mysticism. Jim Younger's hobby in prison was writing verse, and Charles J. Guiteau, who murdered President Garfield, composed a hymn which by permission of the hangman he sang on the scaffold just before the trap dropped.

* See key to abbreviations, p. 11.

	SIG.	LS/DS	ALS *
Billy the Kid (W. Bonney)	$—	$—	$8500
John Wilkes Booth	500	850	2200
Lizzie Borden	200	400	750
Al Capone	175	400	650
Caryl Chessman	50	75	100
Leon Czolgosz	—	5000	—
Emmett Dalton	65	275	600
Grat Dalton	100	350	500
Robert Dalton	100	350	500
John Dillinger	—	300	500
Robert Ford	100	400	650
Lynnette "Squeaky" Fromme	35	100	160
Gary Gilmore	25	40	75
Charles J. Guiteau	35	100	175
Bruno Richard Hauptmann	75	75	150
Frank James	110	250	375
Jesse James	—	3000	6500
Al Jennings	25	55	75
Capt. William Kidd	1000	2000	4500
Jean Laffite	200	650	2200
Nathan Leopold	35	75	125
Richard Loeb	75	150	300
Charles Manson	50	75	175
Florence Maybrick	25	35	65

	SIG.	DS/LS	ALS *
Lee Harvey Oswald	$250	$350	$1200
James Earle Ray	20	35	60
Gilles de Retz	—	2500	3000
Jack Ruby	50	75	200
Marquis de Sade	75	150	300
Sirhan Sirhan	50	200	300
Son of Sam (David Berkowitz)	50	150	350
John H. Surratt	50	150	325
Mary Surratt	—	300	600
Willie Sutton	20	30	40
Prof. John W. Webster	20	35	55
Bob Younger	150	350	650
Cole Younger	75	225	375
James Younger	100	300	350

7. Billy the Kid (W. H. Bonney)

8. Emmett Dalton

9. Robert Ford

10. Grat Dalton

11. Frank James

12. Lynnette "Squeaky" Fromme

13. Charles J. Guiteau

14. Al Capone

15. Capt. William Kidd

16. Bruno Richard Hauptmann

17. Jean Laffite

18. Jack Ruby

19. Willie Sutton

20. James Earle Ray

21. Nathan Leopold

22. Son of Sam (David Berkowitz)

23. Prof. John W. Webster

24. Cole Younger

25. Jim Younger

26. Bob Younger

Royalty

THE SIGNS MANUAL of the great kings and queens have always fascinated collectors. Francis I of France wrote in an elegant, attractive script; Napoleon used a pen like a saber, assaulting the paper with great slashes, often splitting the nib of his quill and splattering his letter with ink. Some of his swashbuckling signatures still glitter with the gold or silver "sand" used to blot them. So hard to decipher is Napoleon's script that one of his generals, it is said, mistook a letter of Napoleon for a battle map.

The Louis's of France employed secretaries to sign for them and even supplied their favorites with *lettres de cachet,* or orders for imprison-

1

1. *Louis XIV of France and his secretary. The secretary has signed at the top and Louis XIV has written "bon" and his signature.*

ment, signed by proxy in blank. All the owner of one of these potent missives need do was fill in the name of an enemy to have him cast in the Bastille.

When the hated Bastille fell, the royal archives of France were looted by the mobs and tens of thousands of letters and documents of the early sovereigns were pilfered, many to be used for wrapping paper or even less refined purposes. So many historic documents poured on the market that scholars took notice and a new era in the history of philography dawned.

Queen Victoria of England was an avid philographer and treasured a letter of George Washington in her personal collection.

See key to abbreviations, p. 11.

	SIG.	DS/LS	ALS *
Albert I (Belgium)	$25	$60	$100
Alexander I (Russia)	50	125	200
Anne (England)	100	300	750
Joseph Bonaparte (Spain)	25	80	85
Carlotta (Mexico)	75	200	450
Catherine de Medicis (France)	125	375	1000
Catherine II, the Great (Russia)	100	225	800
Charlemagne (France)	—	75,000	—
Charles I (England)	125	350	900
Charles II (England)	100	250	750
Charles V (Holy Roman Emperor)	100	250	850
Charles VIII (France)	100	300	1200
Charles IX (France)	85	275	950
Charles XIV (Sweden)	35	150	250
Christina (Sweden)	75	250	900
Edward VII (England)	20	50	50
Edward VIII (England)	20	75	100
Elizabeth I (England)	400	2500	4000
Elizabeth II (England)	100	185	200
Ferdinand the Catholic (Castile and Aragon)	125	400	1500
Francis I (France)	150	500	1250
Frederick II, the Great (Prussia)	75	150	450
George I (England)	50	125	500
George II (England)	40	100	350
George III (England)	50	85	300
George IV (England)	25	50	80
George V (England)	45	75	125
George VI (England)	45	75	125
Gustavus Adolphus (Sweden)	100	275	650
Henry VII (England)	250	500	3000
Henry VIII (England)	400	1100	3500
Isabella, the Catholic (Spain)	100	200	2000
Ivan IV, the Terrible (Russia)	—	750	—
James I (England)	150	300	850

	SIG.	DS/LS	ALS *
James II (England)	$125	$225	$ 650
Josephine (France)	150	350	850
David Kalakaua (Hawaii)	40	250	450
Liliuokalani (Hawaii)	40	250	450
Louis XI (France)	275	650	2000
Louis XII (France)	200	450	1200
Louis XIII (France)	100	150	1200
Louis XIV (France)	75	150	1200
Louis XV (France)	60	125	950
Louis XVI (France)	65	175	800
Maria Theresa (Austria)	50	150	375
Marie Antoinette (France)	150	450	2000
Mary I (England)	325	1200	3000
Maximilian (Mexico)	75	175	300
Maximilian I (Germany)	75	150	450
Mongkut (Siam)	50	150	300
Napoleon I (France)	125	250	5000
Napoleon III (France)	35	75	85
Nicholas II (Russia)	200	600	1000
Pedro II (Brazil)	25	75	100
Peter I, the Great (Russia)	225	500	1250
Philip, prince consort (England)	25	50	80
Philip II (Spain)	65	165	850
Richard III (England)	—	4000	7500
Victor Emmanuel III (Italy)	25	50	125
Victoria (England)	25	75	85
Wilhelm II (Germany)	30	75	180
William I, the Conqueror (England)	—	75,000	—
William III (England)	90	250	800
William IV (England)	20	40	60

THE SIX GEORGES OF ENGLAND

2. *George I*

3. *George II*

4. *George III*

5. *George IV*

6. *George V*

7. *George VI*

England flourished under the benign rule of the six Georges.

THE SIX FAMOUS LOUIS'S OF FRANCE

8. *Louis XI*

9. *Louis XII*

10. *Louis XIII*

11. *Louis XIV*

12. *Louis XV*

13. *Louis XVI*

The six Louis's built a great monarchy and then destroyed it.

14. *Alexander I (Russia), in Russian script*

15. *Alexander I (Russia), Roman script*

16. *Queen Christina (Sweden)*

17. *Charles VIII (France)*

18. *Catherine de Medicis*

19. *Charles IX (France)*

20. *Catherine the Great (Russia)*

21. *Carlota (Mexico)*

22. *Elizabeth II (England)*

23. *Frederick II, the Great (Prussia)*

24. *Ferdinand (Spain)*

25. *Isabella (Spain)*

26. *Anne I (England)*

27. *Charles V (Holy Roman Emperor)*

28. *Charles V, signed in Latin*

29. *Charlemagne (France)*

30. *Charles I (England)*

31. *Charles II (England)*

32. *Francis I (France)*

33. *Frederick II, the Great (Prussia)*

34. *Gustavus Adolphus (Sweden)*

35. *Henry VIII (England)*

36. *Edward VIII (England)*

37. *James I (England)*

38

chère fille, je vous embrasse avec tendresse, et je vous attends avec impatience. rentrez vous embrasse.   josephine

39

40

41

43

42

Marye the quene.

44

45

46

47

48

49

38. *Josephine (France)*

39. *James II (England)*

40. *Marie Antoinette (France)*

41. *Maximilian (Mexico)*

42. *Mary I (England)*

43. *Peter the Great (Russia)*

44. *Philip II (Spain)*

45. *Napoleon I (France)*

46. *William III (England)*

47. *Napoleon I, as Bonaparte*

48. *Victoria (England)*

49. *Victor Emmanuel III (Italy)*

Scientists and Doctors

WHEN I WAS A sophomore in high school, our science teacher, Dr. Lowell C. Frost, wrote to three noted men—Einstein, Edison and Millikan—and asked them to send him a photograph inscribed to the students of Beverly Hills High School They all complied and the three large and stately photographs were framed and hung in the lobby of the school auditorium. Every day after school I went quietly into the lobby and stood in awe and meditation before the signed photos of these three great scientists. It became a daily ritual with me to pay homage to them. Then one day they were missing from the wall and when I inquired about them I learned they were stolen. Even now, almost half a century later, I still feel a keen sense of loss.

1

1. *Albert Einstein, calculations from his Unified Field Theory*

2. *Edward Jenner*

2

The letters of scientists and doctors are nearly always interesting. I once had a letter of Edward Jenner, developer of smallpox vaccine, denying that cow's heads grew from the arms of persons he had vaccinated. Albert Einstein sometimes wrote long letters in humorous verse, and Harvey Cushing often referred to his quest for rare books and autographs.

The great naturalist Charles Darwin, whose letters are today eagerly sought by philographers, always had a keen sympathy for autograph seekers, and never failed to write his name for supplicants. And why not? He was a signature collector himself as a boy.

* See key to abbreviations, p. 11.

	SIG.	DS/LS	ALS *
Alfred Adler	$35	$80	$175
Louis Agassiz	10	25	45
Frederick G. Banting	75	165	250
Christiaan Barnard	12	25	70
Luther Burbank	15	45	80
Marie Curie	85	175	375
Pierre Curie	150	350	750
Harvey Cushing	40	85	175
Charles Darwin	75	210	375
Humphry Davy	30	80	110
Paul Ehrlich	50	100	170
Albert Einstein	75	400	1000
Michael Faraday	20	55	65
Alexander Fleming	25	50	85
Sigmund Freud	175	500	825
Galileo	1500	7000	15,000
W. C. Gorgas	20	60	115
William Harvey	500	2500	7500
Julian Huxley	10	20	30
Thomas H. Huxley	12	30	45
Edward Jenner	150	450	750
Carl G. Jung	40	120	300
Joseph Lister	50	125	225
Charles H. Mayo	25	55	100
Gregor Mendel	200	475	1400
F. Anton Mesmer	80	200	375
Robert A. Millikan	5	18	35
Maria Mitchell	15	35	75
W. T. G. Morton	100	275	550
Isaac Newton	350	650	2500
William Osler	50	200	300
Louis Pasteur	100	170	325
Linus Pauling	7	15	25
Joseph Priestley	100	300	425
Walter Reed	225	575	800
Jonas Salk	5	15	25
Albert Schweitzer	25	65	110
Ignaz Semmelweis	250	600	1800
Lazzaro Spalanzani	90	300	525
Benjamin Spock	3	5	7
Charles P. Steinmetz	40	75	125
Nikola Tesla	25	60	120
Alessandro Volta	65	225	450

3   *Professor Alfred Adler*

4   *Adieu, encore une fois.*
    Ton vieil ami

5

6   *Bien sincèrement à vous*
    M. Curie

7   *agréez, Monsieur, avec mes remerciements*
    mes salutations bien sincères. —
    P. Curie

8   *Charles Darwin*

9   *I suppose you are busy as ever.*
    My wife sends her love to you all.
    Yours ever.
    Alexander Fleming

10

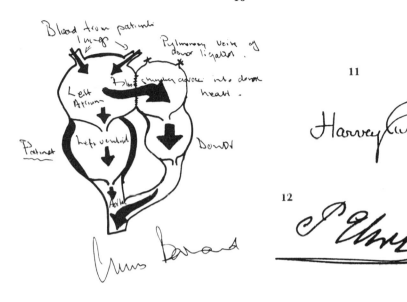

11

Harvey Cushing

12

10. Christiaan Barnard (sketch of heart operation)

11. Harvey Cushing

12. Paul Ehrlich

13. Albert Einstein

14. Humphry Davy

15. Michael Faraday

16. Carl G. Jung

17. Robert A. Millikan

18. Charles H. Mayo

19. Gregor Mendel

20. Maria Mitchell

13   *Albert Einstein. März 1921*

14   *Humphry Davy*   16   *C. G. Jung*

15   *My dear Friend / Yours truly / M Faraday*   17   *Robert A. Millikan*

18   *C H Mayo*

19   *Gregor Mendel*

20   *Maria Mitchell.*

21. *Anton Mesmer*

22. *Isaac Newton*

23. *W. C. Gorgas*

24. *William Harvey*

25. *Joseph Lister*

26. *Jonas Salk (autograph letter signed)*

21

22

23

24

25

THE SALK INSTITUTE

26

1 March 1976

Dear Mrs. Hobson,

I would like to add my congratulations to the many you are receiving on your 100th birthday. To be a centenarian is a rare accomplishment attained by a chosen few. I read of a woman who reached her 100th birthday and said that the reason for her success was that she had learned to cooperate with the inevitable. I am certain this has been true for you as well.

You must have had a large measure of joy and satisfaction in your life, as well as the trials and tribulations of living. I hope you will continue to derive such pleasure as life affords not many more years.

I regret that I cannot be with you on this memorable occasion.

Sincerely,

Jonas Salk.

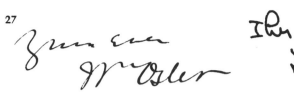

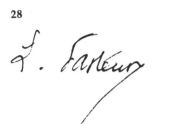

27

28

29

30

31

Baltimore, 1890.

32

33

34

35

36

27. *William Osler*

28. *Louis Pasteur*

29. *Linus Pauling*

30. *Joseph Priestley*

31. *Walter Reed*

32. *Albert Schweitzer*

33. *Lazzaro Spalanzani*

34. *Charles P. Steinmetz*

35. *Nikola Tesla*

36. *Alessandro Volta*

British Authors

REWARD: One million dollars cash for an autograph of William Shakespeare! Surely in some attic or outbuilding in London or Stratford there lies undiscovered at this moment a letter or document signed by the world's greatest writer. Only six authentic signatures of Shakespeare are known, and it is my lifelong ambition to bring the total to seven. But no forgers need apply.

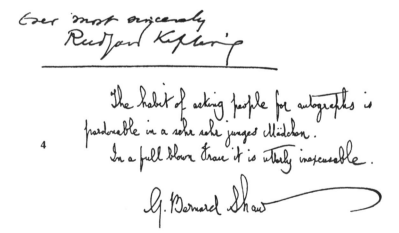

1. *William Shakespeare*

2. *Daniel Defoe*

There are other autographs much rarer than Shakespeare's. Marlowe's, for instance. Only one signature is known of the great dramatic poet, he of the mighty line. Virtually all the leading British authors of the sixteenth and seventeenth centuries left but a scanty supply of autographs, and many eighteenth-century literary autographs also are rare and costly—Defoe's, for example. Not until we reach the Victorian era do we find letters of the outstanding authors available at modest prices.

The hostility of many recent authors to signature seekers is well known in philographic circles. Kipling abhorred autograph hounds. Yet even he relented and mailed me his signature when, as a boy, I sent him in exchange ten cents, my week's salary for hauling out our furnace ashes. That signature today is worth about 250 times what it cost me.

3. *Rudyard Kipling*

4. *George Bernard Shaw (autograph note signed)*

Shaw and Ruskin and Carlyle were notorious for their hatred of signature hunters, but they loathed beggars even more. Sly autograph collectors soon learned how to get dramatic and interesting letters from these literary giants. An appeal for funds for a new church, or a new wing on an old church, would bring an explosive epistle from any of the three, each of whom despised clerics with outstretched tin cups.

A country parson once turned the tables on Shaw. After reading that Shaw was an expert at brewing coffee, the parson wrote asking for the recipe. Shaw sent it, but snidely added, "I hope that this is a genuine request and not a surreptitious mode of securing my autograph." The rector answered, "Accept my thanks for the recipe. I wrote in good faith, so allow me to return what it is obvious you infinitely prize, but which is of no value to me, your autograph."

See key to abbreviations, p. 11.

	SIG.	DS/LS	ALS *
Joseph Addison	$50	$135	$250
Jane Austen	500	1800	6000
Francis Bacon	750	2200	7500
Max Beerbohm	45	110	150
Brendan Behan	50	100	150
Arnold Bennett	15	35	50
William Blake	500	2000	4700
James Boswell	225	375	750
Charlotte Brontë	175	500	850
Emily Brontë	800	2200	6500
Rupert Brooke	150	200	350
Elizabeth Barrett Browning	120	325	475
Robert Browning	50	90	150
Robert Burns	300	775	1250
Lord Byron	175	375	850
Thomas Carlyle	30	100	165
Lewis Carroll	45	110	130
S. T. Coleridge	75	235	425
Joseph Conrad	50	100	160
Noel Coward	15	30	80
Daniel Defoe	375	1800	3500
Charles Dickens	50	110	200
Arthur Conan Doyle	50	125	185
George Eliot	40	65	90
Henry Fielding	400	650	1500
E. M. Forster	15	35	55
John Galsworthy	15	30	50
Oliver Goldsmith	650	2500	6000
Robert Graves	15	30	65
Thomas Hardy	25	45	75
Gerard Manley Hopkins	100	225	·450
A. E. Housman	50	100	165

	SIG.	DS/LS	ALS *
Aldous Huxley	$15	$30	$45
Samuel Johnson	350	850	2500
James Joyce	200	525	800
John Keats	1500	7500	25,000
Rudyard Kipling	25	70	110
Charles Lamb	110	250	600
D. H. Lawrence	75	190	425
T. E. Lawrence	110	250	500
Edward Lear	60	125	225
John Masefield	8	15	20
W. Somerset Maugham	15	35	65
John Milton	1200	10,000	25,000
H. H. Munro (Saki)	50	100	135
Alfred Noyes	7	20	30
Sean O'Casey	30	75	135
Alexander Pope	150	350	700
John Ruskin	25	45	110
Bertrand Russell	15	30	75
Siegfried Sassoon	30	50	85
Walter Scott	35	80	150
William Shakespeare	—	1,000,000	1,500,000
George Bernard Shaw	45	110	185
Mary Shelley	75	200	325
Percy Bysshe Shelley	350	750	10,000
Edith Sitwell	25	55	120
Stephen Spender	20	60	140
Edmund Spenser	2500	10,000	30,000
Laurence Sterne	100	225	600
Robert Louis Stevenson	65	150	235
Bram Stoker	15	30	60
Jonathan Swift	250	650	1200
A. C. Swinburne	50	85	150
Alfred, Lord Tennyson	40	90	135
W. M. Thackeray	50	75	125
Dylan Thomas	85	125	250
Anthony Trollope	45	150	200
Izaak Walton	425	2000	3500
H. G. Wells	10	35	50
Oscar Wilde	65	110	325
P. G. Wodehouse	7	15	25
Virginia Woolf	65	100	185
William Wordsworth	50	175	400
William Butler Yeats	40	85	125

5. *Jane Austen*

6. *Max Beerbohm*

7. *Lord Byron*

8. *Francis Bacon*

9. *William Blake*

10. *Elizabeth Barrett Browning*

11. *Joseph Conrad*

12. *Charlotte Brontë*

13. *Robert Browning*

14. *Thomas Carlyle*

15. *Arthur Conan Doyle*

16. *Robert Graves*

17. *Noel Coward*

18. *Gerard Manley Hopkins*

19. *Charles Dickens*

20. *Aldous Huxley*

21. *Thomas Hardy*

22. *Oliver Goldsmith*

23. *John Keats*

24. *Samuel Johnson*

25. *Edward Lear*

26. *D. H. Lawrence*

27. *W. Somerset Maugham*

28. *John Ruskin*

29. *Sean O'Casey*

30. *John Milton*

31. *Bram Stoker*

32. *Bertrand Russell*

33. *Percy B. Shelley*

34. *Mary Shelley*

35

[autograph note in secretary hand, signed] Ed. Spenser

35. Edmund Spenser (autograph note signed)

36. Stephen Spender

37. Jonathan Swift

38. Virginia Woolf

39. Sir Walter Scott

40. Dylan Thomas

41. A. C. Swinburne

42. Oscar Wilde

43. H. G. Wells

44. P. G. Wodehouse

36

Stephen Spender.

37

Jonathan Swift

38

Virginia Woolf

your most obedt servant
39
Walter Scott

40 *Dylan Thomas.*

41 *Your obedient servant*
AC Swinburne

42

Pray remember me to Mrs Bemroe and your sons, most truly yours
Oscar Wilde

43

Yours sincerely
H. G. Wells

44

P. G. Wodehouse

P. G. Wodehouse

Religious Leaders

WHEN YOU REFLECT that Mary Baker Eddy and Henry Ward Beecher lived their long lives at the same time and only a few hundred miles apart, it seems amazing that Mrs. Eddy's letters are so rare and costly and the Reverend Beecher's so abundant and inexpensive. This curious fact is one of the anomalies which make philography exciting.

1. *Henry Ward Beecher (autograph note signed)*

2. *Mary Baker Eddy*

1

My dear Sir.
I never send my autograph in answer to letters,
Henry Ward Beecher
Jan 14, 1870 —

2

Mary Baker G. Eddy

Many years ago I acquired for $4.50 from a coin dealer two handsome Kirtland (Ohio) Safety Society bank notes, with denominations of $5 and $10, signed by the Mormon prophet, Joseph Smith, and his associate, Sidney Rigdon. These notes were issued by Smith for the use of his

3

3. *Joseph Smith and Sidney Rigdon (signed bank note)*

176

followers and were not backed by gold or United States currency. A government investigation of them forced the Mormons to leave Ohio and flee to Missouri. It occurred to me that since the payment on these notes was guaranteed by the prophet, the Mormon Church in Salt Lake City might wish to redeem them at face value. The church never answered my letter offering the bank notes for sale, but a few years later I sold them for about four times what I had paid.

Today, identical bank notes of Smith fetch $250 or more. From whatever Elysium he now dwells in, the prophet must contemplate with satisfaction the spectacular value of his once despised currency.

Early in 1977 I acquired after a phone call from the owner several letters which I had supposed were penned by the noted Cardinal John Newman, author of the celebrated hymn "Lead Kindly Light." My disappointment was keen when I looked at the writing and signature and

4 *Lead, Kindly Light, amid the encircling gloom,*

Lead Thou me on!

John H. Cardinal Newman

Nov.ʳ 18. 1883

4. *John H. Cardinal Newman (autograph quotation signed)*

discovered they were written by an obscure American bishop, John Neumann, whose name is pronounced the same as the great Cardinal's. I felt fortunate to sell these Neumann letters for a dollar each. My chagrin was great when I learned two months later that the unknown John Neumann had just been canonized, his third miracle verified. I had literally sold a saint for a song.

* *See key to abbreviations, p. 11.*

	SIG.	DS/LS	ALS *
Henry Ward Beecher	$3	$12	$20
Pope Benedict XV	40	75	125
Phillips Brooks	3	8	12
Saint Frances Xavier Cabrini	75	150	500
John Calvin	325	1100	3000
William Ellery Channing (d. 1842)	10	35	60
John Cotton	70	175	325
P. J. De Smet	150	650	1400
Mary Baker Eddy	150	500	825
Jonathan Edwards	100	250	400
John Eliot	200	750	1800

	SIG.	DS/LS	ALS *
Father Edward Flanagan	$10	$20	$35
Harry Emerson Fosdick	3	5	7
George Fox	100	300	650
Billy Graham	3	5	10
Pope John XXIII	30	55	110
Jason Lee	150	700	1100
Saint Ignatius Loyola	2000	8500	30,000
Martin Luther	1000	8000	25,000
Cotton Mather	125	500	1000
Aimee Semple McPherson	15	30	75
Philip Melanchthon	250	750	2500
Saint John N. Neumann	100	350	1200
John H. Cardinal Newman	40	65	100
Norman Vincent Peale	4	10	15
Pope Pius IX	30	50	60
Pope Pius X	30	55	75
Pope Pius XII	20	35	65
Saint Elizabeth Seton	250	1000	2000
Fulton J. Sheen	3	7	10
Joseph Smith	125	400	2000
Francis Cardinal Spellman	3	7	10
Billy Sunday	5	10	20
Emanuel Swedenborg	350	1000	2500
Charles Wesley	50	100	200
John Wesley	100	300	700
Roger Williams	1200	4500	10,500
Nicholas Wiseman	5	10	15
Brigham Young	55	150	500

5. *Phillips Brooks*

6. *Saint Frances Xavier Cabrini*

7. *John Calvin (autograph note signed)*

5

7

6

8 *W^m E Channing*

9 *et sic commendo vos Xno. Aco valete datu in vrbe Romana decima die inini Rener— ac vro yin xpno moslu mem seruet humillimno seruo Ignatino*

10 *Martinus Luther*

11 *Your most humble seruot C Mather.*

12 *Pius PP. X*

13 *Pius PP. XII*
   12 de Enero de 1947

14 *E. A. Seton*

15 *W A Sunday*

16 *Jonathan Edwards*

17 *EM: Swedenborg*

18 *Providence 25 March 1671*
   yor Fijend & Servant Roger Wiljams

19 *John Wesley*

20 *Brigham Young*

8. William Ellery Channing

9. Saint Ignatius Loyola (autograph note signed)

10. Martin Luther

11. Cotton Mather

12. Pope Pius X

13. Pope Pius XII

14. Saint Elizabeth A. Seton

15. Billy Sunday

16. Jonathan Edwards

17. Emanuel Swedenborg

18. Roger Williams

19. John Wesley

20. Brigham Young

Mouth-Watering Monikers

1. *Napoleon I, emperor of France. The creamy pastry bears his name.*

2. *John D. Rockefeller, Sr., oil billionaire. He introduced oysters Rockefeller to epicures.*

3. *Nellie Melba, Australian soprano. She inspired peach Melba, then atoned by inventing Melba toast.*

4. *F. R. de Chateaubriand, French author. Steak Chateaubriand was his contribution to gastronomy.*

5. *A. Brillat-Savarin, author of* The Physiology of Taste. *Savarin coffee and apricot Savarin.*

6. *Earl of Sandwich, English statesman. He invented the sandwich for eating at the gaming table.*

7. *Count Karl R. Nesselrode, Russian diplomat. He concocted the first Nesselrode pie.*

8. *Luisa Tetrazzini, Italian soprano. Chicken Tetrazzini was named for her.*

9. *Courvoisier, keeper of the seals under Charles X of France. He gave his name to the king of brandies.*

10. *Otto von Bismarck, German chancellor. The delicious hors d'oeuvre, Bismarck herring, is his contribution.*

11. *The Duke of Wellington, British soldier. That crusty delicacy Beef Wellington has helped to immortalize the equally crusty duke.*

Continental
Authors

AUTHORS ARE THE MOST put-upon victims of signature hounds. Most are, like Heine, veritable stockpiles of suitable sentiments, or like Hans Christian Andersen, instant producers of amiable verses. But there have been recalcitrants. One who abominated signature seekers was Anatole France. Crafty women laid traps to get a facile epigram from his pen. One matron invited him to a sumptuous banquet and, after the noted author had been seated and served, produced a tablecloth annotated by previous victims and asked Anatole France to add a verse and his signature. France quickly feigned an attack of indigestion, excused himself from the table, and fled from the house.

1. *Anatole France*

2. *Alexandre Dumas, père*

The French are the most delightful of letter writers. Dumas's script is so curvaceous that he could have posed as a bank clerk. Voltaire often signed his handwritten epistles with a chalice-shaped "V." Verlaine's manuscripts are eloquently stained with absinthe. Jean Cocteau loved to make simple sketches signed only with his first name.

Letters and manuscripts of the Russian authors are regarded as national treasures and very few have emerged from Russia. Except for those

3. *Leo Tolstoy (autograph note signed, English script)*

4. *Leo Tolstoy (Russian script)*

181

authors who had a wide foreign correspondence, like Tolstoy, or who lived abroad for many years, like Turgenev, their letters are virtually unobtainable. It's no use searching for those giants Lermontov, Pushkin, Gogol, Dostoevsky and Chekhov in Russia. Their letters and manuscripts are all in official archives. And the few autographs which have escaped to the Western World fetch astronomical prices and are savagely competed for in the auction rooms.

One of the most distinguished philographers of his era was the German poet Goethe, who treasured in his collection several letters written to him by Byron.

• See key to abbreviations, p. 11.

	SIG.	DS/LS	ALS *
Hans Christian Andersen	$150	$250	$425
Honoré de Balzac	60	200	250
Charles Baudelaire	120	200	325
Henri Bergson	15	30	55
Giacomo Casanova	80	350	550
Miguel de Cervantes	—	10,000	15,000
Anton Chekhov	350	1000	2800
Jean Cocteau	30	65	120
René Descartes	600	2600	6500
Fyodor Dostoevsky	300	1500	3500
Alexandre Dumas, père	20	35	45
Gustave Flaubert	30	65	100
Anatole France	10	20	30
André Gide	15	25	40
Johann Wolfgang von Goethe	150	325	750
Nicholai Gogol	300	2000	4000
Maxim Gorki	110	275	375
Jacob Grimm	35	100	200
Wilhelm Grimm	35	100	200
G. W. F. Hegel	125	350	900
Heinrich Heine	200	425	750
Victor Hugo	20	35	65
Franz Kafka	85	200	350
Immanuel Kant	275	650	2000
Selma Lagerlöf	15	25	40
Giacomo Leopardi	50	225	310
Mikhail Lermontov	350	1500	3000
Emil Ludwig	5	10	15
Niccolo Machiavelli	300	750	2700
Thomas Mann	35	100	225
Karl Marx	350	1000	2500

	SIG.	DS/LS	ALS *
Guy de Maupassant	$ 25	$ 45	$80
André Maurois	7	15	25
Ferenc Molnár	15	30	55
Friedrich Nietzsche	300	500	1200
Boris Pasternak	75	135	250
Alexander Pushkin	500	2000	3500
Marcel Proust	75	135	300
Rainer Maria Rilke	65	175	275
Arthur Rimbaud	350	1500	3500
Friedrich von Schiller	250	575	2200
Heinrich Schliemann	25	70	90
Arthur Schopenhauer	225	600	1500
Stendhal (Marie Henri Beyle)	150	400	900
Torquato Tasso	250	800	1800
Count Leo Tolstoy	80	150	375
Ivan Turgenev	50	80	125
Paul Verlaine	100	250	310
Alfred de Vigny	50	100	200
Voltaire	100	225	450
Émile Zola	40	65	125

5

6

7

8

9

5. *Hans Christian Andersen (autograph quotation signed, German script)*

6. *Hans Christian Andersen (Roman script)*

7. *Honoré de Balzac*

8. *Henri Bergson*

9. *Charles Baudelaire*

10. *Miguel de Cervantes*

11. *Giacomo Casanova*

12. *Gustave Flaubert*

13. *Fyodor Dostoevsky*

14. *René Descartes*

15. *Maxim Gorki (Roman script)*

16. *Maxim Gorki (autograph quotation signed, Russian script)*

17. *Jacob Grimm*

18. *Wilhelm Grimm*

19. *Goethe (Roman script)*

20. *Goethe (German script)*

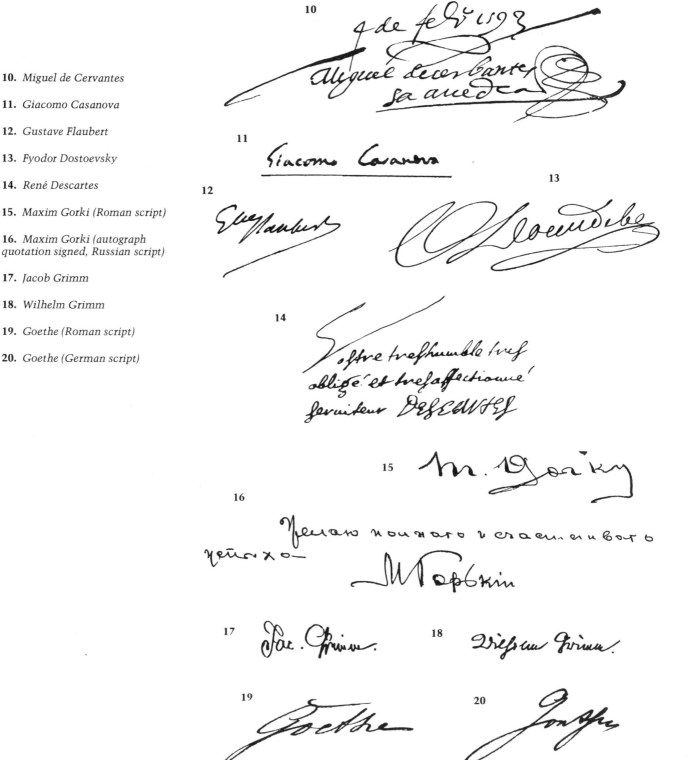

21. *Georg W. F. Hegel*

22. *Heinrich Heine*

23. *Victor Hugo*

24. *Franz Kafka*

25. *Immanuel Kant*

26. *Thomas Mann*

27. *Karl Marx (autograph note signed)*

28. *Friedrich Nietzsche*

29. *Alexander Pushkin*

30. *Arthur Rimbaud*

31. *Heinrich Schliemann*

32. *Rainer Maria Rilke*

33

34

33. *Ivan Turgenev*

34. *Friedrich von Schiller*

35. *Arthur Schopenhauer*

35

36. *Torquato Tasso*

37. *Voltaire (signature, with his title)*

38. *Paul Verlaine*

39. *Stendhal (autograph note signed Henri Beyle)*

40. *Alfred de Vigny*

41. *Émile Zola*

36

37

38

39

40

41

Nazi and
Fascist Leaders

MOST FEARSOME OF ALL RELICS wrought of pen and ink are the letters and documents of the Nazis. They fascinate us by their evil. From the scribbles of the brutal Heydrich to the illegible scrawl of the ferret-faced Goebbels, they appeal to philographers. Strangely, many leading collectors of Nazi autographs are Jewish. The late Philip D. Sang of Chicago, co-founder of the Olin-Sang Memorial Library at Brandeis University, was in-

1

1. *Reinhard Heydrich (autograph note signed)*

2. *Dr. Joseph Goebbels*

3. *Hermann Goering (autograph note signed)*

3

2

trigued by Nazi documents, and I well recall his delight and excitement when he acquired from me the original top-secret Nazi plans for the invasion of Belgium and Holland.

One of the leading Nazi collectors now active, whose family was wiped out in an Austrian concentration camp during World War II, has assembled a most important Nazi collection, including the original appoint-

4

4. *Nazi war criminals: Hermann Goering, Gen. Alfred Jodl, Baldur von Schirach, Joachim von Ribbentrop, Wilhelm Keitel, Erich Raeder, Albert Speer, Constantin von Neurath, Hjalmar Schacht, Fritz Sauckel, Karl Doenitz, Hans Fritzsche, Arthur Seyss-Inquart, Ernst Kaltenbrunner, Walther Funk, Hans Frank, Alfred Rosenberg, Wilhelm Frick and Julius Streicher*

ment of Goering as reichsmarshal of the Luftwaffe, signed by Hitler, which I framed for him with an array of medals such as Goering wore.

Recently I asked a Jewish collector of Nazi memorabilia to explain why he found such grim souvenirs so fascinating. "It's like having the head of the hunter on the wall, instead of the hunted," he said.

During the reign of terror in Germany, the Nazi leaders seldom gave their signatures to applicants. But while in prison at Nuremberg they readily signed their names for American guards and other visitors and it is not unusual to find all the "war criminals" on a single sheet. So eagerly sought was Goering's autograph that many of his prison letters to his wife, Emma, were intercepted by GIs as war trophies.

The collector must be on guard against Nazi documents signed with facsimile signatures printed by lithography. Hitler used such synthetic signatures on awards of the iron cross and other medals, and especially on Christmas and New Year's cards and thanks for birthday greetings. Yet the führer, an autograph collector himself, spurned facsimiles in his personal collection, which included a magnificent handwritten letter of Frederick the Great presented to Hitler by Rudolf Hess.

* See key to abbreviations, p. 11.

	SIG.	DS/LS	ALS	SP *
Italo Balbo	$40	$35	$75	$50
Martin Bormann	60	150	325	300
Walther von Brauchitsch	25	60	80	50
Count Galeazzo Ciano	25	35	60	30
Karl Doenitz	10	40	70	15
Adolf Eichmann	100	200	450	—
Hans Frank	25	50	65	35
Wilhelm Frick	35	85	175	100
Werner von Fritsch	25	65	90	75
Hans Fritzsche	20	35	65	50
Walther Funk	20	50	75	40
Joseph Goebbels	85	275	550	175
Hermann Goering	100	350	700	185
Franz Halder	20	35	70	50
Rudolf Hess	75	200	375	175
Reinhard Heydrich	100	300	675	300
Heinrich Himmler	60	100	350	165
Adolf Hitler	160	250	2500	325
Alfred Jodl	40	85	175	100
Ernst Kaltenbrunner	25	45	80	70
Wilhelm Keitel	40	85	130	110
Albert Kesselring	25	45	80	35
Hans Lammers	20	35	60	35
Robert Ley	25	55	100	75
Benito Mussolini	60	90	250	125
Constantin von Neurath	20	35	65	50
Franz von Papen	15	35	60	25
Vidkun Quisling	45	80	165	200
Erich Raeder	20	45	75	35

	SIG.	DS/LS	ALS	SP *
Joachim von Ribbentrop	$40	$75	$225	$100
Ernst Roehm	50	100	300	125
Alfred Rosenberg	40	50	70	65
Gerd von Rundstedt	45	75	80	70
Fritz Sauckel	30	40	100	75
Hjalmar Schacht	25	35	55	35
Arthur Seyss-Inquart	35	65	175	85
Baldur von Shirach	25	60	85	35
Otto Skorzeny	30	100	200	75
Albert Speer	15	25	35	20
Julius Streicher	45	125	200	110
Dr. Fritz Todt	25	35	60	40

5. *Martin Bormann*

6. *Rudolf Hess*

7. *Adolf Hitler (autograph note signed)*

8. *Werner F. von Fritsch*

9. *Robert Ley*

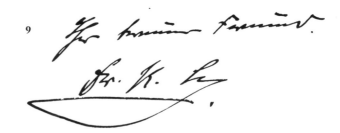

10

11

12

13

14

15

16

17

18

19

10. *Heinrich Himmler*

11. *Gerd von Rundstedt*

12. *Ernst Roehm*

13. *Otto Skorzeny*

14. *Fritz Todt*

15. *Franz von Papen*

16. *Benito Mussolini*

17. *Julius Streicher (German script)*

18. *Italo Balbo*

19. *Vidkun Quisling*

About Charles Hamilton

A collector for more than half a century, Charles Hamilton is the world's most famous autograph sleuth and has helped to send fourteen manuscript forgers and thieves to prison. His impact on philography, or autograph collecting, has been immense. In 1963 he established the first American autograph gallery devoted exclusively to autographs. A scholar with a flare for the dramatic, his frequent clashes with the FBI and Secret Service and his constant, amazing discoveries in the field of documents have made headlines all over the world.

In addition to writing ten books, six of them about autographs, Hamilton has published two pamphlets of poetry, mostly sonnets. His favorite books are the ancient Latin classics. He collects volumes on insects, snakes, outlaws and witchcraft, as well as Roman coins and Napoleonic caricatures.

Of autograph collecting, Hamilton says, "It's the world's most exciting pursuit and belongs to everybody, not just a few highbrows."

Index